No-Nonsense Nutrition in Bite-Sized Portions

---

*Over 50 Articles to Help <u>Anyone</u>
Create an Eating-for–Health Lifestyle*

Kelly Hayford, CNC
Author, *If It's Not Food, Don't Eat It!*

Delphic Corner Press, LLC
Quantity discounts available: 303.746.8970 / info@KellyHayford.com

To receive a free online newsletter on *Eating for Health* and other tips for maintaining a balanced state of well-being, register directly at website: www.KellyHayford.com

Disclaimer: The information contained in this book is for educational purposes only and is not intended to replace or subvert the intervention or participation of a qualified medical professional for diagnosis or disease treatment.

ISBN: 978-0-9765668-1-6
Library of Congress Control Number: 2007909853

in gratitude to...

All those inspired to join me in my mission to help people improve the quality
of their lives through better nutrition — not least of all ourselves.

table of contents

section 4 ~ Eating-for-Health Guideline #4:
Account for Food Allergies & Sensitivities

section 5 ~ Eating-for-Health Guideline #5:
Account for Ailments When Making Food Choices

section 6 ~ Make It So!
Tips for Making Eating for Health a Reality

section 7 ~ Addendum
Assessments & Article Prescription Check List

instructions for use

This book is designed to be used in a variety of ways, by a variety of people. It all began since becoming a nutritional consultant and especially since writing my first book, *If It's Not Food, Don't Eat It! - The No-Nonsense Guide to an Eating-for-Health Lifestyle.* I started to receive more and more requests for articles on specific topics from healthcare practitioners as well as individuals who attended my lectures and classes. I also regularly sent articles to my clients. Fulfilling these requests became so time consuming that at some point I decided to put together a series of articles in one volume to make them easier to pass on to others.

Fashioned after the popular book, *Stretching* by Bob Anderson, this book contains 2-4 page articles that can be read straight from the book or easily photocopied to share with others. Each article takes approximately 5-10 minutes to read. It's a great way for even the busiest or most resistant person to get targeted information about health and nutrition and how to make favorable dietary and lifestyle changes.

how this book is organized
My first book, *If It's Not Food, Don't Eat It!*, provides an overview of the role the food industry and media have played in creating our health-robbing popular food culture. It then offers practical solutions and strategies for change, including five universal *Eating-for-Health Guidelines*. The first five sections of this book are devoted to each of these guidelines. The first article of each provides a brief overview and description of each of the *Eating-for-Health Guidelines*. Subsequent articles are in support of, or somehow related to each specific guideline. Familiarize yourself with this following quick list:

eating-for-health guidelines:

> 1 ~ if it's not food, don't eat it!
> *...and if you do, wait a long time before you do it again so your body can recover.*

> 2 ~ eliminate or relegate stimulants to rare occasions
> *...the more distant and rare the better.*

> 3 ~ eat an abundance of whole, fresh, natural foods
> *...and little to no processed foods.*

> 4 ~ account for food allergies & sensitivities
> *...when making wise food choices.*

> 5 ~ account for ailments
> *...when making wise food choices.*

Section 6 then provides inspiration and practical know-how for implementing the five *Eating-for-Health Guidelines*. Finally, *Section 7* contains health assessments and an *Article Prescription Check List*, which is a great tool for keeping track of which articles you have read or passed on to someone else to read.

protocol suggestions
Many people who have this book will have already read *If It's Not Food, Don't Eat It!* If you haven't already, I highly recommend you do so either before or after you go through this volume. While there is a lot of overlapping information, each book contains more valuable, detailed information that the other does not. Reading and referring to both will give you the most comprehensive experience.

For best results, read through *all* of the following suggestions to generate the most ideas on how you can utilize the information in this book and receive the most benefit. It would also be wise to read or skim through the entire book to get a feel for what's available.

professional healthcare office or classroom setting

Whether you're a medical doctor, chiropractor, massage therapist, acupuncturist naturopath or any other healthcare professional, you can maximize the value of your waiting room by providing access to these articles so everyone can benefit. Implement one or more of the following suggestions:

- *Put copy of book on coffee table in waiting room for visitors to peruse while in the office.*
- *Make multiple copies of one or more articles or health assessments, place in plastic holder for people to take home to read or fill out at their leisure.*
- *Place featured article in double-sided display frame at front desk for people to read while taking care of business. Change monthly or weekly to generate interest and conversation.*
- *Tack article to bulletin board along with supplemental information, photographs or recipes.*

Any of these suggestions can easily be adapted to the classroom environment. In addition, educators can assign specific readings and follow up with group discussions. Healthcare practitioners can start an *Eating-for-Health* support group and do the same.

working with individuals

If you're a healthcare practitioner working with individuals you can assign reading this book from cover to cover at the rate of one article a day, for example. Or, choose specific articles or sections and make copies for them to read in accordance with their particular health issues. Use this easy 5-step protocol to help:

1. *Have patient/client fill out a copy of the* Food Diary Instructions & Form (Section 7) *and the* Symptoms Questionnaire (Section 7) *and return to you at their next appointment.*

2. *Make copy of* Article Prescription Checklist (Section 7). *Based on information gathered, make one cross-mark through each of the top ten priority articles that could benefit that individual.*

3. *Give patient/client 1-3 of these articles at a time along with a specific due date for reading. Put second cross-mark through articles on checklist as they're assigned to keep track.*

4. *Discuss assignments with patient/client, answer questions and give next group of 1-3 articles.*

5. *Have them redo both the* Food Diary *and* Symptoms Questionnaire *in 4-6 weeks after they have implemented changes. Note progress, start again with next level of appropriate articles.*

If you're an individual reading this book and you're not working with a healthcare practitioner, you can coach yourself through this same process. Enroll a buddy to make it fun and hold each other accountable!

basic elimination diet

The *Basic Elimination Diet* is a great tool for identifying food sensitivities, overcoming addictions to extreme foods, developing body awareness, etc. Have clients read each of the seven articles in *Section 4* in the order in which they appear. The last three articles will walk them through the process step by step. The first three articles of *Section 6* would also be helpful. If you haven't done so already, the best way to coach people through an elimination diet is to have done it yourself first so you know what to expect.

cd & books in bulk

This book is also available on CD to make copying and e-mailing articles a cinch. Copies of this book and *If It's Not Food, Don't Eat It!* are also available in bulk at a discount. A growing number of practitioners and educators are making them available to their clients/students with fabulous results. (See last page.)

section one

Eating-for-Health Guideline #1:
If It's Not Food, Don't Eat It!

No-Nonsense Nutrition

Article Series ~ By Kelly Hayford, CNC, Author *If It's Not Food, Don't Eat It!*

Section 1, No. 1

Copyright 2008
Kelly Hayford

If It's Not Food, Don't Eat It!

No-Nonsense Guidelines to an Eating-for-Health Lifestyle

factoid: *An estimated 90% of food budget dollars are spent on processed, packaged food.*

When Betty first started nutrition and health coaching she was taking seven medications, had severe osteoarthritis, could barely walk, was in constant pain and had to catheterize herself daily—among other things. She had heard that making dietary changes could be beneficial to her health, but doubted it could work for her. Betty sought nutritional consulting only because she could no longer afford her medications and her friend had insisted.

Although skeptical at first, Betty was delighted when, in just a few weeks she was able to go off four of her medications, was virtually pain-free, could walk without using her walker, had lost a few pounds, and was generally beginning to feel much better. In addition, her cholesterol had dropped below what it had been when she was taking cholesterol-lowering medications.

What did Betty do to achieve such dramatic results so quickly?

It may surprise you that she didn't cut or count calories, carbohydrates or fat, take a special pill, or start working out. She simply began to switch from the low-quality, chemical-laden processed food brands she had been eating for years, to higher quality, additive-free natural food brands. She also began to include a couple servings of fresh produce into her diet each day.

How can this be so?

This is so because the most popular brands of processed, packaged chemical-laden foods (pseudofoods) so widely consumed today, are injurious to the body. Aside from the *obvious* diet-related conditions such as heart disease, diabetes, or obesity, few people realize poor nutrition in general, is the primary cause of *all* chronic *dis*-ease.

food matters

Like Betty, an increasing number of people are becoming aware of this relationship between diet and *dis*-ease and revamping their diets. Following is a brief overview of five *Eating-for-Health Guidelines* that can help you stay, or get back on the road to health:

1 ~ if it's not food, don't eat it!

The very definition of "food" is that it is *nourishing* to the body. Consequently, anything that is not nourishing to the body (i.e. pseudofoods containing refined sugars, hydrogenated oils, chemical additives, etc.) is not food—don't eat it! And if you do, wait a long time before you do it again so your body can recover.

2 ~ eliminate or relegate stimulants to rare occasions.

Stimulants or extreme foods send your body's chemistry soaring out of balance causing a variety of symptoms including fatigue, brain fog and weight gain. Stimulants include: sugars and other refined carbohydrates (i.e. high fructose corn syrup, white refined flour, etc.), refined salt, caffeine, and alcohol. Less stimulants equal more health and energy.

3 ~ eat an abundance of whole, fresh, natural foods.

Anything that comes in a box, can or package is a processed food (with the exception of some unprocessed brown rice or legumes, for example). Whole, fresh, natural foods (preferably organic) such as produce, meats, fish, poultry, whole grains, legumes and seeds are always your best choice. When you do consume processed foods, natural brand foods are best as they do not contain toxic, chemical additives.

4 ~ account for food allergies & sensitivities when making food choices.

The most common food allergens (i.e. wheat, dairy, soy, corn, etc.) are notorious for causing acid reflux and other digestive problems, constipation, sinusitis, depression, arthritis and more. Most people today are allergic or sensitive to one or more of these foods—and most don't know it! Follow a basic elimination diet to learn which foods may be affecting you.

5 ~ account for ailments when making wise food choices.

There isn't any condition in the body that can't by improved by improving your diet. As you start improving the quality of your diet you'll start feeling better and improving the overall quality of your health. Also, learn which foods exacerbate or help improve any specific conditions in order to give your body every opportunity to heal.

When applied consistently over time, these five *Eating-for-Health Guidelines* produce "amazing" results as Betty can attest. It's miraculous what the body can do when fueled properly—energy is restored, excess weight is shed, body systems are regenerated, disease is reversed, and nagging symptoms disappear.

Where should you begin? Start with the basics: *if it's not food, don't eat it!*

Health-robbing psuedofoods, natural food brands, and whole, fresh, natural foods.

No-Nonsense Nutrition

Article Series ~ By Kelly Hayford, CNC, Author *If It's Not Food, Don't Eat It!*

Eating-for-Health Guideline #1:
If It's Not Food, Don't Eat It!

food (foôd) *n.* 1. any <u>nourishing</u> substance that is eaten, drunk, or otherwise taken into the body to sustain life, provide energy, promote growth, and repair. 2. anything that nourishes.

— *American Heritage Dictionary*

The first *Eating-for-Health Guideline* conjures up thoughts of basic human survival skills. We can all hear the voices of well-meaning adults the world over, grimacing as they tell a small child to take something out of its mouth because it isn't food. This first simple guideline embraces this same notion, addressing what has become a culturally acceptable propensity to eat substances that have been passed off as food, but in fact are not. In a nutshell, the first *Eating-for-Health Guideline* is…

if it's not food, don't eat it!
…and if you do, wait a long time before you do it again so your body can recover.

This guideline makes a crucially important distinction which most health advocates either neglect to mention or fail to emphasize, thus leading to a lack of adequate understanding on the part of the average consumer. In addition, it is a guideline that is relatively easy to implement once you get it and get into the habit of doing it. In fact, I believe that following this first guideline to *Eating for Health* is the very least we can do for ourselves and our families; for to do otherwise is surely the equivalent of eating for *dis*-ease.

I have had countless people report to me that after following this guideline religiously, they dramatically reduced or completely eliminated every conceivable *dis*-ease, including migraine headaches, digestive and eliminative disorders, depression, anxiety, PMS/menopausal complaints, seizures, asthma, and more. Many have also reported that they lost weight (on average about 10 pounds the first month) without decreasing their caloric intake.

it's not food
The obvious first step in understanding this first all-important guideline would be to define what is food and what is not. For the purpose of *Eating for Health*, food is defined as anything Mother Nature created that is *nourishing* and supportive to the human body. Anything that is *not* created by Mother Nature and is *not* nourishing and supportive to the human body is *not* food. This would include, but not be limited to, any of the following:

- *Any synthetic or chemical food additives such as preservatives, artificial sweeteners, artificial flavorings, artificial colorings, anti-caking and thickening agents, flavor enhancers, or any other chemical added to food for whatever purpose.*

Section 1, No. 2

Copyright 2008
Kelly Hayford

- *Any synthetic or chemical substance that has found its way into food by vicarious means, such as growth hormones and antibiotics fed to livestock, pesticides sprayed on produce, and tap water that contains toxic chemicals such as chlorine, lead, arsenic, etc.*

- *Any substance that may have once been considered food, but which has subsequently been processed to the degree that the chemical makeup is so greatly altered it can no longer be considered a real food according to any reasonable standards. For example: white refined sugar or flour, high fructose corn syrup, refined/hydrogenated oils, genetically modified organisms (GMO's), etc.*

In addition to these three categories, the reformulated end product of any processed food that contains any of the above substances would no longer be considered a real food either. It would be considered what I refer to as a pseudofood, fake food, or food item.

why this guideline

Fake-food substances and chemicals taken into the body from our food, water, air and even over-the-counter and pharmaceutical drugs, are *anti*-nutrients. They are called anti-nutrients because they rob our bodies of essential nutrients in several ways.

Anti-nutrients can block nutrients from being absorbed, cause nutrients to be excreted, and burden the body by expending nutrients in an effort to process and detoxify them. They also displace the nutrients that a person would otherwise be getting from quality, nutrient-rich foods.

As for the safety of individual chemicals, FDA approval and the subjective research on behalf of food manufacturers are not reliable. However, if you look at anecdotal evidence and the public sector, which has essentially become a laboratory of sorts, the study that has been taking place over the last few decades in the public laboratory clearly indicates that eating fake foods is detrimental to people's health. In addition to the skyrocketing rates of cancer, heart disease, Alzheimer's, Parkinson's, and other chronic degenerative diseases among adults, the biggest display of the effects these health-robbing pseudofoods are having is on the most vulnerable segment of the American population, our children.

Today's children are the first generation to eat these substances in the amounts and frequency with which they do. In only two decades, in addition to obesity rates having doubled, when you look at the rising numbers of learning disabilities, ADD, ADHD, autism, Type 2 diabetes, depression, suicide and psychosis among our children, it becomes apparent that something is wrong. These are complex issues that, no doubt, have other factors coming into play. However, anti-nutrient, fake foods in combination with a lack of proper nutrients are clearly compromising our children's development and having a catastrophic effect on their general health and well-being.

There is no reason to put these substances in your body. *They're not food—don't eat them!* Stick with whole, fresh, natural foods that have stood the test of time. You can be confident these *real foods* won't harm your body. They will, in fact, nourish and strengthen it. Also take advantage of the many natural-brand processed foods that *don't* contain chemical additives.

No-Nonsense Nutrition

Article Series ~ By Kelly Hayford, CNC, Author *If It's Not Food, Don't Eat It!*

Health-Robbing Things to Avoid

Following is a partial list of some of the most health-compromising substances found in processed foods today. These are all substances that you would be wise to avoid putting in your body at all costs. Unfortunately, popular brand pseudo-foods are filled with them. Eating only natural brand processed foods will greatly reduce the chances of running into these health robbers. These substances are not food, don't eat them!

In brief, the list of things to avoid includes, but is not limited to the following:

- refined sugars
- white refined flour
- refined salt
- the bad fats
- nitrates & nitrites
- sulfites
- monosodium glutamate (msg)
- artificial sweeteners
- artificial colorings, flavorings & preservatives
- pesticides, herbicides, hormones & antibiotics
- genetically modified organisms (GMO's)

The rest of this article will discuss the first four substances that we have mistakenly been led to believe are foods. The rest will be discussed in subsequent articles.

refined sugars

Refined sugars are found in just about every processed food today. As simple carbohydrates lacking in fiber and nutrients, refined sugars are anti-nutrients that deplete the body of vitamins, minerals, and enzymes. Regularly fueling your body with quick-burning refined sugars is associated with numerous health conditions, including major diseases such as Type 2 diabetes, obesity, heart disease, cancer, and osteoporosis as well as lesser *dis*-eases such as fatigue, allergies, PMS/menopausal complaints, digestive and eliminative problems, arthritis, asthma, insomnia, depression, hyperactivity, learning disorders, and more.

Check ingredient labels for sugar and its equivalents, including sucrose, high-fructose corn syrup, corn syrup, dextrose, glucose, fructose, and maltose. And don't be fooled by processed foods you find at the natural foods store that are sweetened with refined sugars such as brown sugar, cane juice (evaporated, dried, raw, or milled), muscovado sugar, Turbinado sugar, Sucanat, or Demerara sugar. Although they are a better choice than those just mentioned, they are still refined sugars and should be consumed only on occasion.

We are sugar-aholics in this country as evidenced by the epidemic proportions of Type 2 Diabetes and pre-diabetes we are experiencing. This is such an important topic there are a couple upcoming articles completely devoted to it that can help you further.

white refined flour

Similar to refined sugars, white refined flour is a simple carbohydrate that quickly breaks down into sugar when consumed. This happens because the refining process has stripped the once whole grain—a nutritious complex carbohydrate that is slowly metabolized by the body—into a simple, refined carbohydrate that is now an anti-nutrient. As such, it will not only deplete the body of vitamins and minerals, but will also raise blood sugar as it is quickly metabolized.

Many food items made with white refined flour also have refined sugar added to the mix, especially breads and other baked goods. Also be aware that many pseudofood products have misleading verbiage on the front label, such as "rich in whole grain" or "made with natural whole grain." A closer look at the ingredients label on the back, however, may reveal "white refined flour," "unbleached flour," or "enriched wheat flour," all of which are refined flour and are best avoided.

refined salt

Refined salt has been processed at very high temperatures and had all the naturally occurring trace minerals removed except for sodium and chloride. Refined table salt is comprised of 99% sodium chloride, plus toxic additives. Sodium chloride causes electrolyte imbalance and prevents nutrients from being transported to the cells of the body, which can cause water retention and inflammation.

Natural unrefined sea salt (*real* salt) on the other hand, contains over 84 essential minerals, including naturally occurring iodine. It helps nutrients to reach the cell interior and does not cause water retention, inflammation, or cravings. Substitute fine or coarsely ground natural *sea salt* available at health food stores, and you will also be substituting health consequences for health benefits.

the bad fats

This group includes *trans fatty acids* or *hydrogenated* fats and oils that are created when manufacturers heat liquid oils at high temperatures or otherwise alter them to extend their shelf life. These man-made fats are found in most processed foods, especially margarine, commercial vegetable oils, peanut butter, roasted nuts, potato and tortilla chips, cookies, crackers, pastries, frosting, salad dressings, and more. Even natural brand processed foods sometimes contain these health-robbing fats. *Fried foods* are also considered bad fats, as frying (cooking fats and oils at high temperatures) creates free radicals that are harmful to the body.

Poor quality fats have been associated with a host of *dis*-eases in the body including cardiovascular disease, obesity, impaired immunity, increased free radical production, increased cholesterol levels, infertility, diabetes, and cancer. In addition, they inhibit the body's ability to make use of the beneficial fats, or essential fatty acids, and are also a major cause of digestive disturbance.

No-Nonsense Nutrition

Article Series ~ By Kelly Hayford, CNC, Author *If It's Not Food, Don't Eat It!*

Harmful Food Additives to Avoid

factoid: *Since the 1950's over 3500 man-made chemicals have found their way into manufactured food. Nowadays in the U.S. alone we consume every year a staggering one million tons of food chemicals.*

—Patrick Holford, *Optimum Nutrition Bible*

There are far too many chemical food additives to list here. Following is the short list of some of the most common and most problematic that would be wise to familiarize yourself with.

nitrates & nitrites
These nasty little toxins are primarily used as color fixatives for processed meats such as bacon, sausage, hot dogs, cold cuts, meat spreads, deviled and cured ham, and smoke-cured tuna and salmon. High levels of nitrates can also be found in vegetables that have been grown in soil heavily fertilized with nitrate fertilizers. The biggest problem associated with nitrates and nitrites is that when they combine with stomach saliva and food substances, they create nitrosamines, which are powerful cancer-causing agents. In addition, many people experience acute reactions to these carcinogens, often in the form of headaches, irritability, or fatigue. There are numerous brands of processed meats readily available at health food stores that do not contain them. These are your best choice when it comes to processed meats—and fresh, organic meats are even better!

sulfites
Sulfites are added to foods as both a color fixative and preservative. The FDA estimates that one out of every hundred people is sulfite-sensitive. Asthmatics are particularly at risk. Reactions range from severe to mild, and may include acute asthma attack, loss of consciousness, anaphylactic shock, diarrhea, nausea, brain fog, muscle aches, headaches, and extreme fatigue. In addition, 17 fatalities occurred as a result of sulfite ingestion before the FDA finally banned the most dangerous uses of sulfites, and set strict limits on other uses in 1986.

Sulfites are still found in a variety of cooked and processed foods, including baked goods, condiments, dried and glacéed fruit, jam, gravy, dehydrated or precut or peeled fresh potatoes (often used to make French fries or hash browns), molasses, shrimp, and soup mixes. They are also in beverages, such as beer, wine, hard cider, and even some fruit and vegetable juices. Many people experience mild to moderate reactions to sulfites contained in processed foods, often without realizing the cause. It is believed that sulfites accumulate in your system over time and, consequently, some people develop reactions later in life.

Dried apricots that are bright orange are the most visual representation of products that contain sulfites, in contrast to dried apricots that do not contain sulfites, which are dark brown and more shriveled. Check ingredients labels for *sulfites, sulfur dioxide, sodium bisulfate,* or *sodium* and *potassium metabisulfite.* Red wine also frequently contains sulfites, and is the reason many people experience an intensified hangover and headache after drinking it.

artificial sweeteners

When it comes to artificial sweeteners—you name it, I don't recommend it. Whether it's Saccharin (*Sweet'n Low*), aspartame (*Equal, Nutrasweet, Spoonful*), sucralose (*Splenda*), Acesulfame K (*Sunette, Sweet One*), each of them is shrouded in controversy and reports of adverse reactions ranging from seizures to headaches to asthma attacks, to liver and kidney damage, and even weight gain. There are so many safe, natural sweeteners , why take the chance?

Contrary to popular belief, there is nothing "diet" about aspartame. In fact, some studies show that diet soda containing aspartame actually causes people to *gain* weight because it is an addictive neurotoxin that induces cravings for snack foods and more artificially-sweetened foods and beverages. Unfortunately, aspartame has been increasingly added to processed foods in recent years, despite the fact that it is the number one most complained about substance to the FDA. This neurotoxin has been banned in Japan and other countries due to its health risks. I have worked with a number of people who have been relieved of a variety of issues, especially depression and anxiety, by going off diet soda that contains aspartame.

monosodium glutamate (msg)

Like aspartame, MSG is also an addictive neurotoxin that accumulates in the tissues, causes weight gain and a host of other problems. Because MSG is so prevalent and so problematic for so many people there are two upcoming articles exclusively devoted to it. For more information on both MSG and aspartame, read: *Excitotoxins: The Taste That Kills*, by Russell Blaylock.

artificial colorings, flavorings & preservatives

Food additives of all kinds have long been suspected, and frequently proven to cause adverse health conditions including cancer, hyperactivity, ADHD, and allergic reactions. All pseudofood products, and many other products such as vitamins, pharmaceutical and over-the-counter drugs, including cold and cough syrups, toothpaste, and even skin care products (60% of which are absorbed through the skin), contain chemical additives that have been linked to numerous health problems. Children are especially at risk due to the smaller, more sensitive nature of their developing bodies, and the fact that most processed junk foods geared to the younger set are loaded with artificial colorings, flavorings, and preservatives.

In the early 1970's, Dr. Benjamin Feingold was one of the first medical professionals to report diminished symptoms of hyperactivity and ADHD in children who eliminated additive-containing foods from their diet, especially artificial colorings. The *Feingold Association* helps children and adults apply proven dietary techniques for better behavior, learning and health. Their website, www.feingold.org, is a fabulous resource. Behavior problems aren't the only health risk associated with food additives, and children aren't the only ones who suffer from their effects. Because of the many health risks posed and general anti-nutrient status, adults and even family pets can certainly benefit from avoiding or better yet, eliminating them altogether.

factoid: *Although many additives are used in very small amounts, it has been estimated that the average American consumes about five pounds of food additives per year. If you include sugar—the food industry's most used additive—the number jumps to 135 pounds a year.*

— Prescription for Nutritional Healing

No-Nonsense Nutrition

Article Series ~ By Kelly Hayford, CNC, Author *If It's Not Food, Don't Eat It!*

MSG: The Hidden Health Robber

Well into my third year of actively making changes to my diet and lifestyle in an effort to improve my failing health, I was still sick and tired all the time. I had recurrent migraines, depression, brain fog, irritability, PMS, mood swings, and *extreme* fatigue after eating—so extreme I often could not stay awake.

It was after one of my unavoidable after-lunch-napping episodes that one of the primary causes of my woes was revealed. A fellow co-worker found me in the break room out cold. I was embarrassed when she woke me up out of what felt like a drunken stupor and asked if I was all right.

I told her how it had become literally impossible for me to keep my eyes open after I ate lunch and dinner, and how I had splitting headaches on a daily basis, that made it difficult for me to function. She listened attentively, then picked up the bottle of popular-brand salad dressing next to my empty lunch containers.

"What do you expect?" she quipped looking at the ingredients label. "This dressing is loaded with MSG. That'll not only give you headaches and put you to sleep, honey—after awhile it'll kill ya!"

"MS … what?," was my response. I was clueless.

Since then I have learned that MSG (monosodium glutamate) is an artificial flavor enhancer. It is also a neurotoxin that is notorious for causing a host of symptoms and sometimes very severe acute reactions in addition to contributing to the development of chronic *dis*-ease.

I immediately eliminated MSG from my diet and not surprisingly, my debilitating fatigue and migraines went with it! The chronic conditions I was experiencing also began to subside.

Millions of people have had very similar experiences, discovering that one or more chemical food additives is the culprit in an acute or chronic condition they have been grappling with and once they removed the offending substance(s) from their diet their symptoms and *dis*-eases went away. MSG is one of the biggest culprits.

things to know about msg (monososodium glutamate)

- Neuroscientists agree that MSG is a neurotoxin, killing brain neurons by exciting them to death.

- Despite the fact that in 1980 MSG was added to the FDA's list of additives needing further study due to the uncertainties that exist, MSG has been increasingly added to food products.

- Studies reveal that when fed to pregnant rats or mice, MSG causes the offspring to suffer from learning disabilities.

♦ In other studies on small animals, MSG has been proven to cause brain damage in the young. As a result, many baby food manufacturers voluntarily removed MSG from their products. However, there are still junior food products and baby formulas on the market that contain MSG. Ironically, many formulas for allergic infants contain larger amounts than the regular formulas.

♦ The leading reaction to MSG, which can take up to 48 hours to appear, is migraine headaches. A fact well recognized by headache clinics throughout the country.

♦ MSG also affects the hunger centers of the brain causing those who eat it to crave more food. That's why food manufacturers put it in their products - it keeps you coming back for more!

♦ MSG also causes weight gain. It is actually fed to laboratory animals to fatten them up for research without increasing their food intake.

When you consider that an estimated 60-90% of processed, packaged foods contain MSG, and the majority of foods eaten in this country are processed, is it any wonder that so many people are sick, tired and overweight?

Despite the fact that food manufacturers disguise this toxic additive under more than 27 different names, MSG *can* be avoided. The best way to do so is to eat primarily whole, fresh, natural foods and the natural food brands that don't contain chemical additives.

symptoms associated with MSG include, but are not limited to:

• headaches/migraines	• lethargy	• dizziness
• weight gain	• pressure around eyes	• anxiety/panic attacks
• extreme fatigue	• blurred vision	• hyperactivity/ ADD
• depression	• runny nose	• behavioral problems
• burning sensation	• sneezing	• irritability/angry outbursts
• numbness/tingling	• shortness of breath	• muscle/joint pain/stiffness
• chest pain/tightness	• asthma attacks	• bloating
• rapid heartbeat	• frequent urination	• nausea
• drowsiness	• seizures	• vomiting
• foggy thinking	• insomnia	• stomach/intestinal cramps
• weakness	• chills and shakes	• PMS/menopausal issues

note: Be aware that Aspartame can cause the same adverse reactions as MSG (monosodium glutamate) in people who are sensitive to them. Both have been shown to kill brain cells and cause subsequent endocrine disorders in laboratory animals. *Acute* reactions to MSG can sometimes take up to 48-72 hours to show up. Chronic conditions associated with MSG develop over time and may take time to reverse. See next article for more on MSG, including resources, remedies and the many names under which MSG may be listed.

No-Nonsense Nutrition

Article Series ~ By Kelly Hayford, CNC, Author If It's Not Food, Don't Eat It!

Section 1, No. 6

Copyright 2008
Kelly Hayford

MSG: Remedies & Resources

factoid: *MSG toxicity is cumulative, so even if you don't react to it immediately, it could still be causing you problems that you're not aware of and won't be aware of for years to come.*

—Marilu Henner

Since starting to educate people about the problems associated with monosodium glutamate (MSG), I have received numerous testimonies and thank you notes from people who have benefited from eliminating processed foods that contain this toxic flavor enhancer from their diet. Although relief from migraines and other headaches are reported the most, many others have reported getting relief from everything from PMS to brain fog to depression to hot flashes by taking this one simple action.

MSG is now estimated to be added to over two-thirds of pseudofood brands. It is primarily found in soups, broths, bouillon, salad dressings, sauces, frozen meals, candy, seasonings, ice cream and candy. Eating whole, fresh, natural foods and purchasing only natural brand processed foods is the best way to avoid it.

Do check labels in the health food stores, however. Unfortunately, I have run across it in a few natural brand processed foods as well, usually listed as "autolyzed yeast extract," or "yeast extract." Although some people may have no reaction to MSG in these forms, those of us who are very sensitive to it may. Also be aware that "natural flavoring" is a catch-all phrase for what is frequently a lengthy list of chemicals which can include MSG.

Commercial dairy products may also cause MSG reactions in MSG-sensitive people because some dairy products are ultra-pasteurized, some are fermented, and many contain additives that are problematic for MSG-sensitive people.

hidden sources of MSG

In addition to being listed outright as MSG or monosodium glutamate, food manufacturers disguise this toxic additive under more than 27 different names.

Terms that *always* indicate MSG:

- monosodium glutamate
- autolyzed yeast
- yeast extract
- hydrolyzed vegetable protein
- hydrolyzed protein
- hydrolyzed plant protein
- plant protein extract
- sodium caseinate
- calcium caseinate
- textured protein
- hydrolyzed oat flour
- potassium glutamate

Terms that *frequently* indicate MSG:

- malt extract
- malto-dextrin
- bouillon
- broth
- stock
- flavoring
- natural flavoring/artificial flavoring
- natural beef or chicken flavoring
- seasoning
- spices

Terms that *may* indicate hidden MSG:

- soy sauce
- gelatin
- carrageen
- enzyme modified

- protein fortified
- fermented
- ultra pasteurized

note: In Europe, E621 is used on labels to signify MSG.

remedies

It is important to understand that MSG accumulates in your tissues. So if you know or suspect you have a sensitivity to it, it would be wise to take measures to cleanse it from your system to help reduce your sensitivity. If you are not currently sensitive to MSG, also understand that because it accumulates in your system there is a good chance that you may become sensitive to it in the future.

For acute reactions to MSG, also known as MSG syndrome, there are a few remedies I have found to be very effective antidotes. Try doing one or all of them at the first sign of a reaction. Find which works best for you:

- ◆ *Drink 2-3 cups a day of spearmint tea.*

- ◆ *Steep 3-4 bags of spearmint tea in a quart of water for 15-20 minutes. Add to a hot bath and soak for 20 minutes.*

- ◆ *Take 50mg of Vitamin B6 three times a day for a couple of days until symptoms subside.*

- ◆ *Irrigate the colon with an at-home enema or have a colonic performed by a licensed colon hydrotherapist.*

Eliminating MSG from your diet and cleansing and strengthening your body in general, will help flush out accumulated MSG from your system and reduce overall sensitivity. There is also an MSG homeopathic remedy available for this purpose. Some speculate that sensitivity to MSG is caused by a Vitamin B6 deficiency. So you may also try taking a quality food-based Vitamin B supplement that contains Vitamin B6 for a few months.

helpful resources

For more information on MSG, consult the following books and websites:

- *Excitotoxins: The Taste That Kills,* by Russell Blaylock ~ www.RussellBlaylockmd.com

- www.MSGTruth.org

- *Battling the MSG Myth* ~ www.MSGMyth.com

- www.HealthDangers.com

- *The Truth in Labeling Campaign* ~ www.TruthInLabeling.org

No-Nonsense Nutrition

Article Series ~ By Kelly Hayford, CNC, Author *If It's Not Food, Don't Eat It!*

Hormones, Pesticides & GMO's

Harmful Substances Used to Produce Our Food

factoid: *Every year a staggering 2.6 billion pounds of pesticides and herbicides are sprayed onto food and pastures.*

pesticides, herbicides, hormones & antibiotics

Although you won't find these listed on an ingredients label, the practice of using pesticides, herbicides, hormones, and antibiotics in agricultural production has become widespread in this country. Unfortunately, it is a practice that is having serious consequences we are only just beginning to realize and understand. Some of these consequences extend far beyond the mere individuals who are consuming the foods produced with these toxic substances; consequences that are upsetting the natural balance of our precious ecosystems and will affect generations to come.

Many plastics, household chemicals, personal care products, and environmental toxins, pesticides, herbicides, hormones, antibiotics and other synthetic drugs, send manmade hormone-disrupting chemicals into our bodies and the natural environment. There is growing evidence that these substances may be contributing to or responsible for recent worldwide increases in health problems, including precocious puberty, breast and prostate cancer, infertility, low sperm counts, auto-immune diseases, and even osteoporosis.

These toxic chemicals are also linked to a host of lesser symptoms and *dis*-eases such as allergies, food intolerances, candida, learning disabilities, PMS, menopausal conditions, and more. In addition, the food industry's excessive use of antibiotics for both therapeutic and livestock growth purposes is contributing greatly to the problem of antibiotic-resistant bacteria and viruses. Toxic chemical pesticides are similarly creating pesticide-resistant bugs.

Less than 100 years ago it took 4-5 years to bring cattle to slaughter. And now, with the help of enormous amounts of corn, protein supplements, and drugs, including growth hormones and antibiotics, it only takes 14 months. When you consider what these aberrant practices are doing to the animals who are subjected to them, it isn't too difficult to imagine the impact these practices could be having on our human bodies and our surrounding environment.

Whether it's animal products or produce, the best way to avoid toxic pesticides, herbicides, hormones, and antibiotics is to eat certified organic foods and those that clearly state on their labels that they do not use or contain these substances. For more information on this topic I highly recommend reading *Our Stolen Future: Are We Threatening Our Fertility, Intelligence, and Survival?* by Theo Colburn. It's a classic well-documented book that presents an eye-opening overview.

factoid: *70% of all antibiotic drugs in the U.S. are being fed to farm animals as growth promoters or production aids, reducing the effectiveness of these drugs in humans and increasing the spread of resistant bacteria.*

genetically modified organisms (GMO's)

You won't find these listed on food product labels either, despite the fact that over 90% of Americans say the FDA should require labeling of genetically modified organisms (GMO's), also known as genetically engineered (GE). Not surprisingly, strong lobbying on the part of the food industry has prohibited such a requirement. This is most unfortunate because GMO's are one of history's most dangerous and radical changes in our diet. Introduced into our food supply in the mid-1990s, these largely unregulated ingredients are now in 60-70% of the foods in the US.

In April 1999, Dr. Arpad Pusztai, a top European GMO safety researcher, publicly revealed that rats fed supposedly harmless GMO's developed potentially pre-cancerous cell growth, smaller brains, livers, and testicles, partially atrophied livers, and a damaged immune system. Within a single week, virtually all major manufacturers committed to stop using GMO ingredients in their European brands.

The biggest problem associated with GM foods we are already seeing in humans is a dramatic increase in unpredictable and hard-to-detect food allergies. In terms of environmental concerns, farmers are finding that the pesticides the bio-tech companies sell to go with the GM crops aren't working. As a result, farmers are actually resorting to older very toxic chemicals.

Even more insidious, genetically engineered organisms cross-pollinate with other non-GMO crops and the subsequent transmutation is irreversible. This is alarming when you consider that the long-term consequences for both humans and the environment are, as yet, not fully known. What is eminently clear, however, is that there are problems—potentially catastrophic problems—associated with these Frankenfoods, as opponents often call them, and further testing and regulation are needed. The damage that may be done is irreversible and has the potential to affect every living creature on the planet.

In addition to the health hazards, the biotech industry is undermining the livelihoods of farmers the world over, forcing them to purchase their patented seeds year after year, and suing them for exorbitant amounts if they don't. The practice of planting saved seed is a practice as old as farming itself; a practice that is a necessity for many farmers, especially those in underdeveloped nations who cannot afford to purchase new seed every year.

To avoid contributing to the unscrupulous endeavors of the biotech industry, and keep your family and the environment safe, once again, consume foods that are truly organic and clearly state that they use *non*-GMO ingredients.

helpful resources

Educate yourself further on this important topic by consulting these valuable resources:

- www.OrganicConsumers.com ~ for information on the bio-tech and organic industries

- www.TheFutureOfFood.com ~ features a fabulous documentary entitled: *The Future of Food*

- www.ResponsibleTechnology.org ~ for online shopping guides, how to get involved, and the books, *Genetic Roulette: The Documented Health Risks of Genetically Engineered Foods* and *Seeds of Deception*, both by Jeffrey M. Smith, and more.

No-Nonsense Nutrition

Article Series ~ By Kelly Hayford, CNC, Author *If It's Not Food, Don't Eat It!*

Making the Transition to Natural Brand Foods

Anyone can easily make the transition away from eating anti-nutrient psuedo-foods by merely switching the *brands* of foods they regularly eat to natural food brands. This is the very least that anyone can do for themselves in terms of *Eating for Health* and is a cinch to do these days. The health food industry now provides a growing supply of organic produce that is grown without toxic pesticides and herbicides; free-range and organic meat, fish, poultry and dairy products without synthetic growth hormones and antibiotics; and processed foods that do not contain chemical preservatives, additives, or hydrogenated oils. They can be found at recognized natural foods stores and co-ops, and at an increasing number of regular chain grocery stores usually placed in sections designated as "natural" foods.

Keep in mind that taste is acquired and if you've been eating brands that contain chemical additives, especially artificial flavorings and high amounts of sodium, sugar, etc., your taste buds have acclimated accordingly and may be burned out to some degree. Whereas some of you may not be excited about the taste of a natural food brand counterpart when you first try it, over time you will acclimate to them and start enjoying them more and more. Eventually you will find the former foods offensive. This can take some time. Many of you will like the taste of the natural food brands right from the start, sometimes even better than the fake-food brands you had been eating!

Either way, countless people who have made this one simple change in their diet have come back to me later and testified that they have more energy, mental clarity, balanced moods, have lost weight, are in less pain, are sleeping better, stopped having headaches, and more.

Nevertheless, I realize the thought of making this transition may still be a little uncomfortable. Many have confided to me that they have never been in a health food store, aren't familiar with natural food brands, and find the whole business a little intimidating. If you feel this way, get creative and courageous. Enroll a friend, child or family member to embark on this adventure with you (preferably a willing one). Many natural foods stores arrange store tours. Call your local store for details. You can also ask a friend or family member who is a self-avowed health food nut (I'm sure you know at least one!) to accompany you on your first trip to the health food store. Most would be thrilled to help you.

If you do not have health food brands available in your town or the selection is limited, once again, get creative. First, look to the surrounding areas and consider driving a little distance. Plan ahead and stock up on non-perishable items. You can then supplement with fresh produce and meats from your local grocery store. If your local grocery store doesn't carry any of the additive-free brands mentioned, request that they do. Given enough requests, they are bound to start carrying at least some of them. Many natural foods can now be purchased online. Check out www.NaturalGrocers.com.

If you don't have a health food store in your area, chances are you live in rural America. If that is the case, start asking around for farms in your area that have antibiotic and hormone-free fresh meats, poultry, eggs and dairy products that they make available direct to consumers. Remember *Eating for Health* is an adventure. You will be meeting new people, going new places and otherwise creating a whole new life for yourself in unsuspecting ways.

clear your kitchen

There are basically two ways to clear your kitchen of all pseudofoods and make way for a healthier eating lifestyle. Each has its benefits and drawbacks. You must decide which is best for you.

1 ~ the clean sweep

Schedule 1-2 days for this project. Make a clean sweep of all pseudofoods in your kitchen placing them in boxes as you go along. Drop off at your local food bank. Next, go to a natural foods store and replace these fake foods with their natural brand equivalents and whole, fresh, natural foods.

The payoffs for making a clean sweep are big and immediate. Over the next few days and weeks, your energy will increase and your body will start to feel better in many ways. I don't know anyone who has done a clean sweep that has ever regretted it. You dramatically improve your health and increase chances for success, just by taking this one simple step. The time and money it takes to get the job done are, of course, the two biggest challenges with this approach. Depending on the size of your family and how much food needs to be replaced, it can cost up to several hundred dollars and take 1-2 days, as mentioned.

2 ~ replace products one by one

Replace non-food items with natural brand processed foods one-by-one as you run out. Obviously this will take some time and you probably won't get the quick and unmistakable improvements in your health and energy, as these changes will occur more gradually. Enthusiasm may also wane, and there is a chance you may abandon your efforts before you ever get to experience the benefits. The uspide is that you won't have to invest an initial chunk of time and money as you do with the clean sweep.

Doing at least a partial clean sweep of all salty snack foods and sugary treats would be wise. Having them around is too much a temptation for most people, and constantly indulging in them is what perpetuates food cravings and addictions more than any other single factor.

natural food brands

Some popular natural food brands include, but are not limited to:

Alta Dena	Eden Foods	Lundberg Farms
Amy's	Fantastic Foods	Newman's Own
Annie's Naturals	Garden of Eatin'	Pamela's
Arrowhead Mills	Hain	Seeds of Change
Barbara's Bakery	Health Valley	Shari's Organic
Bearito's	Horizons	Shelton's
Bob's Red Mill	Imagine Foods	Spectrum Naturals
Breadshop	Kettle Chips	Westbrae

No-Nonsense Nutrition

Article Series ~ By Kelly Hayford, CNC, Author *If It's Not Food, Don't Eat It!*

Dietary Basics

We are all aware that there is much debate over questions regarding portions, frequency of meals, how much protein versus carbohydrates, to eat meat or not to eat meat, etc. The *Dietary Basics* presented here provide a framework from which to work, while allowing enough flexibility to account for individual needs. For example, amounts are expressed in a range to account for different body weights (i.e., smaller amounts for children, mid-range for teens, larger amounts for adults) and also to allow for varied individual needs (i.e., someone trying to balance blood sugar may need protein 3 times a day, while someone else may only need 1 serving a day, etc.). It is important to find what is right for *your* body at this time in your life.

Regarding servings or portions, this is another area of nutrition that is fraught with confusion. It all starts with the fact that the words *serving* or *portion* are general terms with no universally accepted measurement. To make things easy, the best approach to serving size is in the palm of your hand, literally.

Lay out your hand flat with fingers together. There's your serving size for a piece of fish, chicken, steak or other animal protein. Curl your hand into a fist and there's your serving size for grains, a snack or a piece of fruit, give or take a little. Hand sizes vary according to the size of the person. So do appropriate serving sizes. Smaller people have smaller hands and therefore should eat smaller servings. Bigger people have bigger hands and therefore should eat bigger servings. Makes sense, doesn't it?

People who are in sync with their natural biological needs do this instinctively, especially those who eat primarily a whole foods diet. You may already be doing this and just never noticed or thought about it. If you are not, emotions, addictions or food allergies may be overriding your natural inclinations. You may also be eating too many processed foods, which can also interfere.

As you read through the *Dietary Basics*, make a mental note of those you are already implementing, and others which you may be going overboard on or missing altogether. Then experiment by following the recommendations and find what works for you within them. Keep in mind as you are experimenting and making changes that discovering what really works for you is a process that can take time.

Be conscious that what you may currently consider to be working for you may be just what you're *used* to and your body has become chemically addicted to, so when first making changes, you may feel worse before you feel better. Given adequate time and effort, however, you will find that adopting a new way of eating works even better for you once you have successfully moved through the initial transition period.

Biochemical imbalances caused by years of eating in a way that did not support and nourish your body may require short-term measures to restore equilibrium.

Once equilibrium has been restored, a more balanced way of eating may be adopted. For example, if someone has been eating copious amounts of meat for many years, they may do well to not have any meat for a period of time to clear and strengthen the digestive tract. Once their system has cleared, they may then return to eating meat in more moderate amounts.

Similarly, those who have been eating way too many sweets and have developed imbalanced blood sugar would be wise to refrain from all sweets, including fruits, until their blood sugar levels are stabilized. The same would be true of fats, and extreme or stimulant foods. Start experimenting within the parameters of the following *Dietary Basics* and you will soon discover what's right for your body-mind system.

dietary basics

1 ~ follow the eating-for-health guidelines
...*as much as possible.*

The *Eating-for-Health Guidelines* are truly the cornerstone of any health- promoting diet. In a nutshell, the five guidelines to *Eating for Health* are:

1 ~ If it's not food, don't eat it!

2 ~ Eliminate or relegate stimulants to rare occasions

3 ~ Eat an abundance of whole, fresh, natural foods

4 ~ Account for food allergies & sensitivities when making food choices

5 ~ Account for ailments when making food choices

2 ~ drink plenty of pure water daily
...*in accordance with your body's needs (approximately half your weight in ounces).*

3 ~ eat 2-4 pieces of fresh fruit a day
...*preferably local, organic and in season.*

4 ~ eat 5-9 servings of fresh vegetables a day
...*preferably raw or lightly steamed.*

5 ~ eat 1-3 servings of protein a day
...*animal or vegetable protein, or alternate.*

6 ~ eat 1-3 servings of complex carbohydrates a day
...*either whole grains or starchy vegetables.*

7 ~ consume good fats (essential fatty acids) daily
...*either 1-3 tablespoons "good" oil, ground seeds or an EFA supplement.*

8 ~ eat a variety of different foods
...*for a wide spectrum of nutrients and to reduce sensitivities.*

For more details on the Dietary Basics, read: *If It's Not Food, Don't Eat It! - The No-Nonsense Guide to an Eating-for Health Lifestyle,* by Kelly Hayford, CNC.

There isn't any condition in the body that can't be improved by improving your diet!

No-Nonsense Nutrition

Article Series ~ By Kelly Hayford, CNC, Author *If It's Not Food, Don't Eat It!*

Healthy Habits

Follow these healthy lifestyle habits regularly to reverse or prevent future *disease*, increase energy or find and maintain your natural weight:

1 ~ eat only when hungry
  ...and under optimal conditions.

Keep your digestive fire burning. Put too many logs on the fire, or food in your stomach as the case may be, and you will stomp out your digestive processes. Good digestion is a key ingredient to optimal health and energy. Allow at least 2-3 hours between meals or snacks and don't eat for at least 2-3 hours before going to bed. It is also wise to eat only under optimal conditions, not when hurried, stressed, or excessively fatigued.

2 ~ don't drink beverages with food
  ...thereby diluting the digestive juices.

Drink beverages at least 15-30 minutes before meals or snacks on an empty stomach and not for at least a ½-1 hour after eating. This will ensure that digestive juices such as saliva, enzymes and hydrochloric acid are not diluted, which can impede proper digestion.

3 ~ chew, chew, chew
  ...to ensure adequate mastication and saliva secretion.

It is important to remember that the first step of digestion occurs in the mouth through chewing and the secretion and subsequent mixture of saliva with the food. Food should be chewed (masticated) to a pulp in order for it to be of the finest consistency before entering the stomach and also to allow for adequate saliva secretion.

4 ~ follow food-combining principles
  ...whenever possible to ensure proper digestion.

Because different foods require different digestive juices and enzymes to digest them, food combining is a way of supporting this natural biological system of processing and assimilating foods. Food combining is a fantastic way to improve your digestion and elimination, lose weight, and increase your energy. There are a few different schools of thought and entire volumes written on this topic. We will keep things simple here by introducing just the basic rudiments of this practice:

1. *Eat fruits alone on an empty stomach and wait at least 15 minutes before eating something else.*
2. *Vegetables may be eaten with proteins or starches.*
3. *Proteins and starches are best eaten at separate meals.*
4. *Or, if proteins and starches are eaten at the same meal, layer them by eating the protein first, then vegetables, then the starchy food.*

Section 1, No. 10

5 ~ follow the body's natural cycle

...eat your biggest meal at noon and don't eat after 6-7:00 p.m. or at least 2-3 hours before bedtime.

Eat your biggest meal of the day at noon when your digestive machine is at its peak operation. Eat your evening meal no later than 6-7:00pm. And do not eat for at least 2-3 hours before going to bed so as not to disrupt sleeping patterns. This will also give the body adequate rest and time for the digestion and assimilation process that takes place at night.

6 ~ cleanse regularly

...to clear and strengthen your entire body.

It is a long held notion among natural health advocates that toxins and chemicals can be stored in the tissues and organs of the body wreaking havoc with your health. This is very common, especially in our culture with its poor eating and lifestyle habits and the added burden of environmental toxins and consumption of large quantities of chemicals in the form of over-the-counter and pharmaceutical drugs. For this reason, it is a wise practice to cleanse and rejuvenate the body on a regular basis, and especially if you want to prevent the onset of, or are already experiencing any ill health.

7 ~ troubleshoot digestion & elimination

...to maintain health and keep things running smooth.

Gas, bloating and belching are all signs of poor digestion, which leads to poor elimination, which leads to poor health! For this reason, it is important to follow the preceding *Healthy Habits* in order to achieve optimal digestive and eliminative function on a regular basis. If you do get constipated, *don't* allow the waste to continue to back up. If things are really backed up, consider taking some herbal cleansing formulas or colon irrigation. You may also go on a *Basic Elimination Diet*, eat minimally, or drink only liquids (clear vegetable broths, etc.) until the colon clears and digestion improves. Definitely make use of temporary measures, but for long-term results, adopt new habits that will eliminate the cause.

8 ~ exercise & de-stress regularly

... to keep all body-mind systems working optimally.

Get yourself moving, breathing, stretching, and relaxing on a regular basis. These are not luxuries of life. They are necessities. So, indulge often. If you don't have things that you like to do already, explore what's available by taking advantage of free introductory classes offered at dance, yoga, and martial arts studios. And don't forget about walking, one of the best exercises and de-stressors that's absolutely free. When you find a thing or two you like, stick with it. Enlist a buddy to go with you to increase the fun and likelihood of it actually happening.

No-Nonsense Nutrition

Article Series ~ By Kelly Hayford, CNC, Author *If It's Not Food, Don't Eat It!*

Bottled Water:
Full of Health or Full of Hype?

factoid : *An estimated 25-40% of bottled water is merely tap water .*

With widespread reports of dangerous pathogens, toxic flouride and chlorine—and yes, even pharmaceutical drugs!—coming out in our tap water, it's not surprising that bottled water is the fastest growing segment of the overall beverage industry. Sales have tripled in the last decade and now exceed over $15 billion per year. Fifty-four percent of all Americans drink bottled water.

But is this often high-priced commodity really the best choice when it comes to fulfilling our daily H2O quota? Or has over half the population fallen prey to yet another marketing extravaganza? Unfortunately, there is not a simple yes or no answer. There are multiple factors to consider when it comes to making wise decisions about what kind of water to drink.

First, there are a few basic categories or types of bottled water available on the market today. From mineral to artesian water, each usually has one or another purported health benefits associated with it. Whether or not the health benefits associated with these types of water are valid or not is the topic of much debate among health professionals, with no definitive answers.

Regardless of any potential health benefits that may be associated with any given type of bottled water, the most important thing for people to know is that all brands are not created equal.

Although there are pure, high-quality bottled waters available (see other side), deciphering the good guys from the bad can be tricky. Due to substandard and challenging government regulations, what it says on the label outside the bottle is not always what's inside.

For example, a study done by the *Natural Resources Defense Council* (NRDC) found that an estimated 25% of bottled water tested is really just tap water in a bottle! Other sources claim as much as 40%. Check the label for the words "municipal source" on the ingredients label to know.

In another example, 500,000 liters of *Coca-Cola's Dasani* brand water was recalled in Britain due to high levels of bromate, a carcinogenic chemical. Pathogens can also be a problem as the NDRC further reports that one-fifth of the bottled waters tested exceeded unenforceable state or industry bacteria guidelines.

Other concerns voiced by those in opposition to the proliferation of this industry include: the 1.5 million tons of plastic used for bottling and the toxic chemicals released into the environment during this process; possible consumption of toxic chemicals leached from the plastic bottles; a tremendous amount of plastic added

Section 1, No. 11

Copyright 2008
Kelly Hayford

to landfills; and a tremendous amount of resources expended in the overall production, packaging and transportation of bottled water products.

All things considered, in conjunction with the NDRC, I recommend water filtered at the source either through a quality in-home filtration system or one available at most natural foods stores, as the safest and usually most economical overall drinking water for daily consumption.

fruit & vitamin waters

One of the growing trends in bottled water is fruit- and vitamin-enhanced waters. They *sound* like an easy way to pack in more nutrients, but in actuality don't provide any true health benefits. The quality of these products is based on the quality of the water and the substances added. Consumers seem better off with a natural mineral water than drinking added synthetic isolated nutrients.

Fruit waters should not be considered a substitute for drinking water. They're officially categorized as beverages by the FDA and should be treated accordingly. As with any beverages, sugar content should be taken into account. Keeping in mind that 4 grams=1 teaspoon of sugar can be helpful when making choices.

recommended drinking water

for every day use...

Fill 5-gallon plastic water jugs weekly at a water dispenser kiosk that uses a *reverse osmosis* filtration system. Short of installing a similar system in your home, this is the purest water you can get at the most economical price. Fill smaller, reusable water containers when going out. Although some recent reports voice concern about the blue, hard-plastic used for water bottles, I still believe that purified water is a much better choice than drinking from the tap. We have to be realistic, glass bottles are always best but for most people the larger bottles at least, are weight prohibitive.

for super hydration & special needs...

My favorite bottled water is *Penta* water. Special processing gives this water 16x faster hydration than regular water. Not surprisingly, it is the preferred water for many Olympic athletes, is a must for those with kidney stones, those undergoing chemotherapy treatment, and more. It also comes in bottles made of safe plastic! To learn more, visit: www.PentaWater.com

for a refreshing treat...

Instead of flavored waters that contain sweeteners and/or other questionable ingredients, I recommend *Metromint* water—my other favorite water. The original flavors, peppermint and spearmint, are great for digestion, hot summer days, and even menopausal hot flashes! The new lemon and orange flavors are refreshing and healthful as well. To learn more, visit: www.Metromint.com

section two

Eating-for-Health Guideline #1:
Eliminate or Relegate Stimulants to Rare Occasions

No-N☺nsense Nutrition

Article Series ~ By Kelly Hayford, CNC, Author *If It's Not Food, Don't Eat It!*

Eating-for-Health Guideline #2:
Eliminate or Relegate Stimulants to Rare Occasions

factoid: *...coffee, tea, chocolate, white sugar, alcohol, artificial sweeteners and pre-servatives and salt and tobacco. It takes little awareness to realize that the effect of most of these is as stimulants, not nutrients. They are used to whip an overloaded liver and/or stressed adrenals into one more round of struggle. Unfortunately, their end result is to cause further weakness of these organs as well as thoroughly irritating the stomach.*

— Jon Matsen, N.D., *Eating Alive*

Simply stated, *Eating-for-Health Guideline #2* is:

eliminate or relegate stimulants to rare occasions
   ...the more distant and rare the better.

All stimulants or extreme foods send your body's chemistry soaring out of balance, then crashing in the opposite direction in an effort to restore balance. The sound and image of a bomb dropping—*phhheeeeeeoooooow--boom!*—is the best way to describe what takes place in the body when stimulants are consumed. This is a good thing to keep in mind when deciding whether or not to indulge in them.

In terms of foods and beverages, stimulants include, but are not limited to:

- *Sugars – including refined carbohydrates (high fructose corn syrup, white refined flour, etc.) and all other concentrated sweeteners*

- *Refined Salt*

- *Caffeine & chocolate*

- *Alcohol, tobacco*

- *MSG, artificial sweeteners, preservatives*

These extreme substances are anti-nutrients that act more like drugs than food in the body and as such, could also easily be included in the first *Eating-for-Health Guideline*. Like drugs, they are notorious for being addictive in nature and the dramatic internal upheaval they induce can cause acute and chronic reactions ranging from mild to severe. In general, stimulants are the biggest robbers of energy, mental clarity, and your taste buds.

You won't believe how much better food will taste once you have been off them for awhile. They also alter your natural instincts, causing unnatural cravings. For example, no one would even think about sitting down and eating a whole bag of apples or slamming six glasses of water, but how many of you have ever eaten a whole box of cookies, or drank a six-pack of beer in one sitting?

In addition, all stimulants have a dehydrating effect on the bile, blood, and digestive juices, which can interfere with all bodily functions. But most importantly, regular consumption of stimulants over time weakens and degenerates the body, the manifestation of which can develop into a variety of chronic symptoms and *dis*-eases.

problems associated with stimulants

Depending on the stimulant(s) of choice and individual variances, the symptoms and dis-eases associated with regularly eating stimulants includes but is not limited to the following:

- lowered immune function
- adrenal exhaustion
- fatigue
- insomnia
- anxiety
- depression
- mood swings
- PMS/menopausal issues

- cancer
- heart disease
- high cholesterol
- sinusitis
- allergies
- edema
- inflammation
- arthritis

- tooth decay
- kidney & liver problems
- hypoglycemia
- digestive disturbance,
- candida *(yeast over growth)*
- headaches
- high blood pressure
- and more!

If that's not reason enough to eliminate stimulants altogether or only have them on rare occasions, I don't know what is!

Although the concept of eliminating stimulants from your diet might be pretty straightforward, the actual process of eliminating them may not be as easy. In fact, out of all the guidelines this may be the most difficult to implement for the majority of people for three main reasons.

First these extreme foods are often the focal point of social functions, such as cake and ice cream at birthday parties, cocktails and salty snacks before a holiday dinner, doughnuts and coffee during a business meeting, etc. Second, most people are addicted to one or more of them, which makes going off of them a process they don't understand or never get around to. And finally, people frequently underestimate the toll stimulants are taking on their health and energy, and consequently have no desire or motivation to eliminate them from their diets. I guarantee, however, that if you do eliminate extreme foods or have them only rarely, your life will change in ways you never thought possible.

go for the ferris wheel

Imagine for a moment that you were forced to ride the high speed, thrills-'n-spills roller coaster over and over again every day a few times a day. You could get confused, exhausted, irritable, or sick to your stomach just thinking about it, and those are only the immediate effects. Yet that's exactly what people do when they regularly consume stimulants, as we have discussed.

Now imagine if instead, you rode on an even paced, old-fashioned Ferris wheel each day. You rode around only once in a 24-hour period, and the easy ebb and flow of the ride coincided with your natural sleep/wake cycle, feeling tired when it was time to go to bed, sleeping soundly through the night, awakening refreshed and feeling energized throughout your day, until the evening when your energy naturally began to taper off. This is the kind of ride you can expect when you either eliminate stimulants altogether, or when you keep the stimulants in your diet under control instead of letting them control you.

People frequently dismiss the notion of cutting out the extreme foods in their diet because they mistakenly believe these stimulating substances are giving them energy. In fact, they're what is depleting many people's energy in the first place. Carole is one such example. When she first came to an *Eating-for-Health* program, Carole announced that she wanted to increase her energy and lose

at least 5-10 pounds. She had revealed earlier that she drank a cup of coffee every morning "to get her going" and drank 1-2 caffeinated sodas to "get her through the day." When I suggested that letting go of these beverages would restore her energy and also help her to lose the weight she had desperately been trying to lose, she vehemently opposed the idea.

"Are you crazy?" she blurted out. "There is no way I am giving up my coffee or soda. They are my only source of energy. If I don't have them every day I can barely function I'm so tired. And since when does cutting out coffee or soda help with losing weight? I never heard that before."

I explained to Carole that she was riding the double-whammy roller coaster of sugar and caffeine, and that the longer she continued on this ride, the worse she would feel over time. I encouraged her to forget about intellectualizing the matter and put it to the test instead. I challenged her to go off the coffee and soda for one week, starting on a Friday so she would have the whole weekend to lay on the couch as she would undoubtedly need to do, while her body withdrew from these drug-like beverages. I promised her that if she pushed through this initial withdrawal period that by Monday or Tuesday she would be feeling better than she had felt in years. Not totally convinced, she said she'd think about it.

When Carole walked into the room for class the following week I could tell by the look on her face that she had done more than think about it. She kept smiling at me and could barely contain herself when it was her turn to give her report for the week.

"Well," she began, "I took the challenge and quit drinking coffee and the colas. By Friday night I thought I was going to die. The only thing that kept me from having a soda to get some relief was that I kept remembering you saying that I might feel this way, and to just drink a lot of water, rest as much as possible, and go through it to get to the other side. By Sunday I started feeling better and then, oh my gosh! Ever since then I have had so much energy I'm driving my whole family crazy cleaning and doing things! You were right, I feel better than I have in years. But what's even more surprising is that I lost five pounds! I have been doing everything under the sun to lose five pounds for the past four years and nothing has worked. I just can't believe it!"

Inspired by the results of quitting caffeine, the following week Carole decided to quit eating refined carbohydrates. She did this by simply switching from the *white stuff* (i.e., white sugar, bread, and pasta) to the *brown stuff* (i.e., whole grain bread, pasta, and natural sweeteners). In just one week she felt even better and lost the other five pounds she had been trying to lose. Like Carole, most people are excited to discover that they can regain their health and energy, and lose weight without resorting to restrictive fad diets they could never maintain, and often compromise their health in the long run.

lowered immune function

In addition to lack of energy and excess weight, the other common consequence of extreme food consumption that people are often not aware, is lowered immune function. Many have taken me up on the challenge

The closer a food is to its whole, fresh, natural state, the higher its nutritional value.

to significantly reduce or cut stimulants out of their diet completely and haven't had a cold, flu, hay fever, sinus infection or other immune-related condition since.

One such person was a woman who came to me because she was having recurrent bouts of bronchitis and wanted to boost her immune system. She had a relatively healthy diet compared to most, eating a wide variety of whole grains, vegetables, and organic animal proteins. Her one downfall, which is common, was sweets. Although she made most of them at home with whole grains and natural sweeteners, it was the fact that she was consuming them daily that concerned me. It's important to understand that even natural sweeteners can be detrimental to the body. As per my recommendation, she went off the sweets and, not surprisingly, got rid of the bronchitis. She also gained two unexpected bonuses: the hay fever she'd had since she was a child never showed up that Spring and she lost ten pounds.

Another woman who took this challenge was a Harvard Medical School professor who participated in a teleclass I offered. She was astonished at her firsthand experience of this phenomenon. Although her medical training had, of course, mentioned that refined carbohydrates suppressed immune function, she had never given it much thought. After all, refined carbohydrates are as commonly accepted as paper napkins in America today. Not even doctors have been able to escape from this pervasive aspect of our popular food culture. After a class in which I talked about the immuno-suppressive nature of refined carbohydrates and encouraged the program participants to put my assertions to the test, she decided to try it for herself.

"I didn't have any refined carbohydrates for a whole week," the professor reported. "Then on Friday, I decided to have my usual bagel before my morning run. It was amazing. I could actually *feel* my immune system weakening as I ate it! I ate it anyway, but it changed my perception of refined carbohydrates forever. During my run that day I felt like my feet were dragging and I tired easily." Her highly-prized Harvard education rightfully provided her with this same information, but it was her own body's experience that spoke to her the loudest, which is usually the case.

Although we have talked a lot about the effects of sugar here, it is important to remember that *all* stimulants create a severe imbalance in the body and deplete the body of vital nutrients; and are subsequently capable of causing the same, or similar symptoms and *dis*-eases in the body. That's why it is crucial, whether you want to reverse an undesirable condition in your body or head one off at the pass, that you implement this all-important guideline to *Eating for Health*. Read on, as the next few articles will help you do just that!

factoid: *Refined sugar, coffee, tobacco, tea, chocolate, alcohol, drugs, and emotional excitement can raise the blood sugar levels and help us to feel good. The problem is that the pancreas and liver will immediately try to decrease the sugar to a lower level. The resultant drop in blood sugar results in a craving for more sweets, coffee, alcohol, cigarette, drugs or emotional tirades.*

—Jon Matsen, N.D., *Eating Alive*

No-Nonsense Nutrition

Article Series ~ By Kelly Hayford, CNC, Author *If It's Not Food, Don't Eat It!*

Breaking Free of Stimulants
Implementing Eating-for-Health Guideline #2

Implementing *Eating-for-Health Guideline #2: eliminate or relegate stimulants to rare occasions,* is often easier said than done. Because of their stimulating nature and powerful ability to dramatically alter one's blood chemistry, stimulants can be highly addictive due to the body's need to continually bring balance to the severe imbalance they create.

For this reason, whether it's sugar or other refined carbohydrates, coffee, chocolate, alcohol, refined salt, or any combination of the lot, going cold turkey in a calculated manner is usually the best way to break such addictions. Going on a *Basic Elimination Diet* as outlined in *Section 4,* can help you through the process.

In a nutshell, you will want to give yourself at least a couple of at-home days to rest, alert all household members, throw out any temptations (people who are serious about breaking their addictions do not leave a stash in their cupboard!), drink lots of water, and sweat it out.

For some, the withdrawal process will be uneventful. For others, it may be rough for anywhere from two days up to a week or two depending on the severity of the hold these addictive substances have on you. You may feel extremely tired, nervous, irritable, and have stomach or headaches during the withdrawal phase. However, I guarantee that you will be so glad that you went through it, because increased energy, mental clarity, a heightened sense of taste and loss of many symptoms (including weight loss) await you on the other side. Isn't experiencing a few days of withdrawal symptoms better than an ongoing life of miserable ailments and no energy?

Once you have restored balance to your body, you may be able to consume stimulants on rare occasions. I use the word *may*, because many people *may not* be able to for quite some time, if ever, as it will send them spiraling back into their imbalanced addictive state. Notice also that I did not use the popular, yet meaningless term, "in moderation" here. I used the word *rare*, which has a different meaning altogether and is important to clearly define.

rare (râr) *adj.* 1. infrequently occurring, uncommon, unusual. 2. highly valued due to uncommonness; special.

— *American Heritage Dictionary*

When it comes to translating the word *rare* on a personal level with regard to the consumption of stimulants, use this definition to guide you while simultaneously taking into account your own personal tolerance level to each individual stimulant. Everyone's tolerance level will be different depending on their weight, overall constitution, level of activity, and current state of health. If symptoms start to return, you have exceeded your tolerance level. In which case, going back off the stimulants before they take over your energy and your life is the best plan.

Section 2, No. 2

Copyright 2008
Kelly Hayford

There isn't any condition in the body that can't be improved by improving your diet!

48-hour test

Unfortunately, many people believe that they are not being affected by the stimulants they consume regularly. They believe that stimulants either don't pose a threat in general, or that they personally are somehow immune to the ravages of these health-robbing substances. If you are one of these people, forget about all the studies you may have read in favor of their consumption, or even anything I have said here, and let your body speak to you. It is there that you will uncover the most powerful evidence one way or the other.

In order to do this, take the 48-hour test. Start by completing the *Symptoms Questionnaire* in *Section 5*. Then, for the next 48 hours eliminate all stimulants in your diet: caffeinated foods and beverages, sugar (including natural and artificial sweeteners), chocolate, salt and alcohol, and any foods that contain them. Remember that sugars and caffeine have been increasingly added to foods, so check labels carefully. Or better yet—eat only whole, fresh, natural foods that don't sport man-made labels. At the end of the 48 hours retest by once again filling out the *Symptoms Questionnaire*. If after 48 hours of being stimulant-free you feel either significantly worse or significantly better, one or more of these buggers is undoubtedly running you.

If, on the other hand, you do not experience any noticeable difference in how you feel, keep in mind that whether or not you are currently exhibiting any effects, stimulants are not good for any-*body*. They undermine health over the long haul and it's probably just a matter of time before regular or excessive consumption of one or more of these decadent delights catches up with you.

Remember that food is something that is *nourishing* to the body. Stimulants are not foods, they do not nourish the body. They are, in fact, damaging and depleting to the body-mind system. As the body weakens and the adrenal glands become exhausted from imbibing in these extreme substances, it takes more and more sugar, cups of coffee, shots of alcohol, and bars of chocolate to get the same high you used to get with just a little; until eventually you won't get a high at all, but will instead be in a constant state of down and out.

Upcoming articles will provide you with more information on individual stimulants, including healthier alternatives. Once again, at first these healthier alternatives may not have the same pizzazz as the real stuff, but give them a chance. Your taste buds will soon adjust to the natural flavor of foods, and the old junk foods you used to hanker for will lose their appeal. The health, energy, and sense of well being that you will experience once you are stimulant free will be well worth any adjustments you may initially have to undergo.

quick reference ~ implementing eating-for-health guideline #2

- *Break free of dependency on stimulants by eliminating them completely until balance is restored.*

- *Then, have extreme stimulant foods only on rare occasions according to your tolerance level.*

- *If symptoms return, eliminate completely once again to restore equilibrium. To expedite the process, drink plenty of water and follow the Basic Elimination Diet for a few days.*

- *Switch from the health-robbing "white stuff" (refined carbohydrates) to the nutrient-rich "brown stuff" (complex carbohydrates). Substitute fruits and natural sweeteners for refined sugars and artificial sweeteners.*

- *Substitute herbal teas or roasted grain beverages for coffee or caffeinated tea.*

No-Nonsense Nutrition

Article Series ~ By Kelly Hayford, CNC, Author *If It's Not Food, Don't Eat It!*

The Sugar Beast
Why You Want to Conquer It & How to Do It

factoid: *Americans consume 53 teaspoons of caloric sweeteners per day, the equivalent of a 5-pound bag of sugar every week and half – 75% more than in 1909. In Europe and North America, fat and sugar count for more than half of all caloric intake.*

— World Watch Institute

We have become a culture of sugar-aholics and the far-reaching ramifications of this burgeoning addiction are only just beginning to be seen. Type 2 diabetes, formerly known as adult-onset diabetes because it rarely struck those under 50, is now in epidemic proportions among both adults and children. Other conditions and diseases associated with excess sugar and junk-food consumption are also skyrocketing, including asthma, heart disease, obesity, cancer, osteoporosis, candida, PMS/menopausal symptoms and more.

It is said that if white refined sugar were put before the FDA today it would not be approved. Unfortunately, white refined sugar and other refined sugars are a multi-billion dollar industry that isn't going away any time soon. Refined sugars are found in just about every processed food today.

As simple carbohydrates lacking in fiber and nutrients, refined sugars are anti-nutrients that deplete the body of vitamins, minerals, and enzymes. They also cause a dramatic rise and rapid fall in blood sugar levels. Eating these simple carbohydrates is like driving a car with a stuck accelerator: you speed around for a short time, then run out of gas.

excess sugar = one of your worst enemies!

It is important to understand that the word 'sugar' refers to two different things. The most common definition of sugar is the white granular substance made from sugar beets or sugar cane, otherwise known as table sugar or white refined sugar. But the word sugar also refers to any of a class of water-soluble crystalline carbohydrates having a characteristic sweet taste. In this case, we find it listed on the back of food ingredient labels as the macronutrient 'sugar,' for example. With this broader definition in mind, sugar includes or is contained in the following:

- fresh & dried fruit
  ...such as apples, pears, oranges, figs, dates, etc.

- processed sweeteners
  ...such as white refined sugar, high-fructose corn syrup, etc.

- concentrated natural sweeteners
  ...such as honey, maple syrup, fruit juice, etc.

- white flour & other refined carbohydrate products
  ...such as white pasta, bread, crackers, etc.

- all alcoholic beverages
  ...including beer, wine and hard liquor.

Section 2, No. 3

Copyright 2008
Kelly Hayford

refined sugar...

...is an <u>anti</u>-nutrient stimulant that is over 99% pure calories—no vitamins, minerals, fiber, or proteins. Regularly fueling your body with quick-burning refined sugars is associated with numerous health conditions, including almost every major disease. Refined sugar is known to cause or contribute to:

- suppressed immune function
- osteoporosis
- asthma, hay fever, sinus congestion
- cancer
- tooth decay
- accelerated aging
- digestive disorders
- arthritis
- hyperactivity & learning disabilities
- candida albicans (*yeast overgrowth*)
- heart disease
- kidney damage
- food allergies/sensitivities

- eczema, acne & other skin problems
- atherosclerosis
- frequent colds & flu
- loss of enzyme function
- liver & gallbladder disorders
- diabetes
- migraines
- blood clots
- depression & anxiety
- mineral deficiencies (*esp. chromium, copper, calcium and magnesium*)
- weight gain & obesity
- PMS & menopausal symptoms

Check ingredient labels for sugar and its equivalents, including sucrose, high-fructose corn syrup, corn syrup, dextrose, glucose, fructose, and maltose. And don't be fooled by processed foods you find at the natural foods store that are sweetened with refined sugars such as brown sugar, cane juice (evaporated, dried, raw, or milled), muscovado sugar, Turbinado sugar, Sucanat, or Demerara sugar. Their names may convey a healthier image and they are a much better choice than white refined sugar or high-fructose corn syrup, for example, but these are all still concentrated, processed sugars and should be kept to a minimum.

When you do indulge in sweets, stick with the natural sweeteners listed in *Section 3* as much as possible , keeping these to a minimum as well. Excess sugar of *any* kind is harmful to the body.

factoid: *Two cans of soda (24 tsps. of sugar) depletes the immune system by 92% for up to 5 hours.*

white refined flour—the *other* sugar

Similar to refined sugars, white refined flour is a simple carbohydrate that quickly breaks down into sugar when consumed. Remember the experiment you did as a kid in elementary science class when you took a bite of a Saltine cracker, and held it in your mouth to see what would happen?

What happened was the taste went from a salty cracker to sweet as sugar within seconds; the lesson being to demonstrate how quickly white refined flour and refined grains break down into sugar.

This happens because the refining process has broken down and stripped the once whole-wheat grain, a nutritious complex carbohydrate that is slowly metabolized by the body, into a simple, refined carbohydrate that is now an anti-nutrient. As such, it will not only deplete the body of vitamins and minerals, but will also spike blood sugar levels as it is quickly metabolized.

Many food items made with white-refined flour also have refined sugar added to the mix, especially breads and other baked goods. In addition, white refined flour is processed with toxic substances such as bleach (how do you think it gets white?) and has a high gluten content which is problematic for a growing number of people. You made paste out of white-refined flour, not whole wheat flour, for a reason. With its fiber removed and gluten remaining, white-refined flour is the perfect ingredient for making a sticky paste that is great for childhood art projects, but not so great for trying to process through your body. For all these reasons, white-refined flour and other refined grains are included in the stimulant category.

As you start to move away from food products made from white refined flour, be aware that because it is a simple carbohydrate, much like sugar, white refined flour can be addictive in nature. You may need to clear it from your system in order to eliminate cravings.

Also be aware that many pseudofood products have misleading verbiage on the front label, such as "rich in whole grain" or "made with natural whole grain." A closer look at the ingredients label on the back, however, may reveal another story. Many will list as the first ingredient either "white refined flour," "unbleached flour," or "enriched wheat flour," all of which are refined flour and are best kept to a minimum

be sugar wise

- When checking food labels, keep in mind that 1 teaspoon = 4 grams. So if a snack bar contains 24 grams of sugar, for example, that would be the equivalent of 6 teaspoons of sugar. Would you sit down and eat 6 teaspoons of sugar at one time? Think before you eat!

- On processed food labels, ingredients are listed in order of their volume in the product. Food manufacturers some times use a combination of sweeteners. Each then appears further down the list making it look as though it contains less sugar than if one sweetener was used and appeared at the top of the list. Check for these hidden sweeteners.

beware artificial sweeteners

Aspartame is a neurotoxin that accumulates in the tissues over time and has been associated with a host of symptoms, including: headaches, depression, fatigue, anxiety, seizures, brain fog, and more. For more on this topic, read: *Excitoxins*, by Russell Blaylock. Similarly, sucralose, saccharin—and all other artificial sweeteners all have controversy and problems associated with them. Be safe rather than sorry and stick with the natural sweeteners.

alternatives to refined sugar:

better:

Sucanat, rapadura, agave, barley malt, brown rice syrup, fruit juice, date sugar, raw honey, *real* maple syrup, molasses & xylitol

best:

Fruit - Nature's sweet treat
Stevia - natural herbal sweetener
(more on stevia in Section 3)

The closer a food is to its whole, fresh, natural state, the higher its nutritional value.

You are what you eat and you are also what you don't eat—eat well, be well.

factoid: *Please, please, stop looking for a way to have lots of sweets without consequences…There's nothing "normal" or "natural" about eating a lot of sweet stuff; the typical American intake of sweets, is nothing short of pathological, and changing sweeteners doesn't make it any more normal. We need to get back to the notion of a "treat" being something that we have on special occasions, not something we have every day.*

— www.HoldTheToast.com

licking the sugar habit

Imbalanced blood sugar is one of the primary causes of fatigue, brain fog, cravings, depression, irritability, weight gain, weakened immune system and more. To help balance blood sugar levels and kick the sugar habit…

- *Follow Eating-for-Health Guideline #2 regularly (i.e. eliminate or relegate stimulants to rare occasions, including:* caffeine, chocolate, refined salt, alcohol and refined carbohydrates (sugars, high fructose corn syrup, white refined flour, etc.)

- *Be aware that going "cold turkey" on refined sugars may cause withdrawal symptoms (headache, fatigue, irritability, etc.), plan ahead, alert household members, drink lots of water, and eat nutritious foods to ease the process. Health, energy, and balanced emotions await you on the other side!*

- *Transition from refined sugars to naturally-sweetened treats.*

- *Take a generous dose of a barley grass green-food supplement daily to help balance blood sugar, reduce cravings for sweets, and provide essential vitamins and nutrients.*

- *Feed cravings for sugar and sweets with protein*

- *Eat protein before sweets to lower overall glycemic index and help stabilize blood sugar.*

- *Have nothing sweeter than fruit during the week. Limit treats made with concentrated sweeteners to a once a week planned indulgence on the weekend.*

- *Eat animal protein or whole grains within an hour of waking up.*

factoid: *Once you decide to kick the sugar habit, you'll notice that your taste buds will start picking up flavors and sensations you may have never experienced before. Everything you eat will start to taste better and more alive in its flavor.*

— Marilu Henner

recommended resources

- *Sugar Blues*, by William Dufty

- *Lick the Sugar Habit*, by Nancy Appleton

- *Little Sugar Addicts: End the Mood Swings, Meltdowns, Tantrums, and Low Self-Esteem in Your Child Today*, by Kathleen Desmaisons

- *Sugar: The Sweet Thief of Life*, article from www.TheDoctorWithin.com

No-Nonsense Nutrition

Article Series ~ By Kelly Hayford, CNC, Author *If It's Not Food, Don't Eat It!*

Section 2, No. 4

Copyright 2008
Kelly Hayford

Alternatives to Coffee

factoid: *Studies show conclusively that caffeine contributes to anxiety, irritability, panic attacks, depression, and anger. With high levels of caffeine in your blood, even the small annoyances of life can gain tragic proportions.*

…what you get from caffeine is really not energy; it's metabolic and neurological stress. Caffeine is, after all, a psychoactive drug, (which) is poisonous. Caffeine is considered harmless simply because it is so widely used. About 80% of American adults drink 3-4 cups of coffee each day.

— Stephen Cherniske, *Caffeine Blues*

Although coffee has become a staple in the average American diet, as the second *Eating-for-Health Guideline* indicates I highly recommend eliminating coffee and other caffeinated beverages from your diet, or having it only on a rare occasion in tolerable amounts.

Caffeine is a stimulant that taxes your adrenal glands, upsetting your energy levels and the overall chemical balance of your body. It has been linked to a variety of detrimental health conditions including high blood pressure, nervousness, fibroids, PMS, menopausal complaints, depression, depletion of vitamins and minerals, and more.

Caffeine is extremely addictive and once hooked, most people have great difficulty breaking away. Refer back to *Breaking Free from Stimulants* for help in this department. To avoid headaches gradually decrease the amount of coffee you drink by 50% each day. You might also like to read and follow the protocol for withdrawal outlined in the book *Caffeine Blues*, by Stephen Cherniske.

Many people tell me that the thing they like most about coffee is the comforting warmth it provides. So, finding a healthier alternative is a great place to start. There are a variety of teas and roasted grain beverages that serve as tasty substitutes for coffee. You may even find that you like one of them even better than that old cup of java (which in my opinion leaves something to be desired in the taste department anyway). Following are some favorites:

- India Spice Tea, Cocoa Spice Tea & Green Tea Kombucha
  all by the Yogi Tea Company

I love all the teas by this company, but these 3 are my favorites. The Yogi Tea Company also offers quite an array of medicinal teas, high quality teas that are worth exploring.

- Bengal Spice & Roastaroma
  by Celestial Seasonings

These two caffeine-free teas are both very flavorful and satisfying. The *Celestial Seasonings* boxes they come in are beautiful and offer inspiring thoughts as well.

- **Kukicha (twig tea)**
  by Eden Foods, Inc.

This Japanese favorite contains a bit of caffeine and is therefore a good stepping-stone for those who experience harsh withdrawal symptoms, such as headaches, when going off coffee. It is also available in a caffeine-free version. It is best simmered for up to 20 minutes to bring out its full flavor. When steeped it tends to be a little weak.

- **Kaffree Roma**
  by Worthington Foods

An instant, caffeine-free roasted grain beverage made with malt barley and chicory, this is about as close as you can get to coffee when it comes to taste. In fact, when I served it to some unsuspecting habitual coffee drinkers, they thought it was instant coffee!

- **Cafix**
  by InternNatural Foods

Cafix is very similar to *Kaffree Roma*, but with added rye and beetroots. This drink has the added benefit of the cleansing and detoxifying power of the beetroots. So go easy to start. For some people it may get your bowels moving a little too much. For others, especially those who rely on caffeine for this same effect, it's perfect.

- **Teeccino**
  by Teeccino Caffé, Inc

Teeccino is a blend of herbs, grains, fruits and nuts that are roasted, ground and brewed just like coffee. Dark, rich, and full-bodied, Teeccino brings you all the satisfaction of a robust brew with no caffeine reaction.

fresh ginger tea

2-3 - ¼" slices fresh ginger
2-3 cups purified water

Combine ingredients bring to a boil and simmer for 20-30 minutes. Serve hot.

factoid: *A few weeks or months after quitting, most people come to realize that they feel much better without the coffee habit. Then most people can enjoy a cup of coffee on occasion when a boost is really needed, without triggering a recurrence of the craving that one feels when it is consumed regularly.*

— Michael Traub, N.D.

tips & tidbits

Add rice, oat or almond milk instead of cream or cow's milk to teas and coffee substitutes. To sweeten, add a small amount of stevia, *real* maple syrup, agave, or raw honey instead of refined sugar. Or drink plain and enjoy the natural taste. If you have any health conditions, try herbal teas with therapeutic properties that address your specific issues.

Curb & Conquer Food Cravings

factoid: *Overwhelming food cravings are the culprit behind every obese body, every broken diet, and every dietary-related disease. If we can stop the food cravings, the unhealthful eating habits will disappear.*

— Doreen Virtue, *Constant Craving*

There are many factors that can contribute to or cause food cravings and addictions. However, whether they arise from imbalanced blood sugar, which is often the case with sweets, food intolerances, nutritional deficiency, or in reaction to stimulants, such as caffeine, or neurotoxic additives such as MSG or aspartame, with rare exception, all food cravings and addictions stem from improper nutrition.

Even what is labeled emotional eating is most often caused by emotional imbalance, which was caused by biochemical imbalance, which was caused by improper nutrition. It *is* about the food. Understanding this is the first step toward freeing yourself from sometimes irrepressible desires for specific foods and even food in general.

Food cravings are your body's way of speaking to you. And although you're hearing these messages loud and clear, you must learn to *accurately* interpret them. Once again, while each message may relate to a specific factor, the bottom line is that food cravings are your body's way of begging you to feed it properly, and it won't stop begging until you do. It's that simple.

quote: *So many of our mistakes come from misinterpreting what our body is trying to tell us…Even if you are not willing to do what you know your body is asking of you, tell yourself the truth anyway. This is the beginning of gaining skill. Awareness is the key to change.*

— Grace Purusha, *The Five Essential Laws of Eating*

give me nutrients or give me death!

Processed foods of one kind or another are eaten excessively in this country, and in some cases, exclusively. This habit more than anything will cause your body to beg the loudest. You may interpret these messages as a desire for more of these foods, but in fact, your body is screaming for more *nutrients,* not more bad foods.

The most poignant and concise explanation for how anti-nutrient, fake foods affect our appetite and create an insatiable desire for them is explained in the book *Fit for Life II.* In this sequel to the classic and highly recommended book *Fit for Life,* authors Harvey and Marilyn Diamond explain:

> *The appestat is an organ located in the base of the brain. It is something like a thermostat. The appestat is responsible for your appetite. It constantly monitors the bloodstream for nutrients. When they are not present in the necessary amounts, you feel hungry. So what do you think happens when*

No-Nonsense Nutrition

Article Series ~ By Kelly Hayford, CNC, Author *If It's Not Food, Don't Eat It!*

food that has had its nutrient content destroyed? You fill up, but because the food is "empty" the appestat registers that you need still <u>more</u> food. You keep eating and eating but the appestat just doesn't turn off. The result is that familiar complaint, "I eat all the time but I'm still hungry." The body is tricked into thinking it needs more food when it's actually crying out for nutrients. Sadly, there is a beneficiary of this tragic situation — the people making and selling you the empty foods! Your apparently insatiable appetite is a result of the most detestable kind of manipulation of your body chemistry imaginable, and it's all done to increase profits while diminishing your health.

In the now famous documentary *Super Size Me*, viewers see this phenomenon unfold before their eyes as Morgan Spurlock develops strong cravings for the McDonald's pseudofood he has committed to eating exclusively for thirty days. This fantastic film is a must-see for everyone, especially those who have an affinity for fast food.

factoid: *Instead of being eaten when we are physically hungry, food is now consumed to satisfy artificial cravings generated by a brain that isn't working right and whose receptor sites beg for synthetic stimulation from chemicals. We eat, but we're never satisfied. We're full, but we aren't contented.*

— Carol Simontacchi, *The Crazy Makers*

play a little game with yourself

Most people who are having problems with food tend to spiral down into thinking something is wrong with them. As you begin to understand the internal machinations taking place in your body such as those just described, you will also begin to understand, as I did, that there is nothing wrong with you. There is something wrong with the food you're eating.

Having this understanding will help you to become a third-party observer to the powerful, seemingly uncontrollable forces of food cravings and addictions. Which is something around which you can play a little game with yourself. A little game that could go something like this: first notice that you're feeling like you could strangle somebody for a piece of chocolate, soda, cup of coffee, etc., or find yourself frantically rifling through the cupboard where you're praying you will find a forgotten candy bar or bag of cheese puffs. Then STOP!

Take a deep breath, center yourself and say, "Gee, isn't it interesting that I could strangle somebody for a little ol' piece of chocolate, soda, cup of coffee, etc. " Or "Gee, isn't it interesting that I am rifling through the cupboard like a maniac looking for anything I can get my hands on that will suppress this unrelenting desire I am experiencing." Then ask yourself, "What's my body *really* trying to tell me?"

Playing this little game with yourself will help you to stop operating on automatic pilot, and if you're lucky, will also at times stop you from nose diving into injurious foods with reckless abandon. But the most important thing you can do to help overcome irrepressible food desires is to start nourishing your body properly. Giving your body adequate amounts of the nutrients it requires and eliminating problematic foods is paramount to reducing and clearing unnatural food cravings and addictions.

quote: *Eating unnatural substances brings about unnatural appetites that can never be satisfied.*

— Grace Purusha, *The Five Essential Laws of Eating*

specific cravings

You may want to review *Eating-for-Health Guidelines #2 and #4* regarding stimulants and common food allergens, as these are some of the most notorious culprits when it comes to food cravings and addictions. As for stimulants, in addition to the problems they present that you have already learned, consuming these substances can set up an imbalanced internal chemistry that makes you crave other stimulants. For example, eating sweets can lead to cravings for salt and vice versa. So staying away from these extreme foods in general is wise.

Staying away from pseudofoods in general, especially those containing MSG and aspartame in particular, is also wise. These neurotoxins are known to induce cravings not only for more of the foods that contain them, but for other poor-quality foods as well.

As for cravings for specific foods, they can be an indicator of specific nutrient deficiencies. Cravings for fatty foods such as potato chips, milk, cheese, ice cream and the like, can be an indication that you're not getting enough essential fatty acids. Because it is so bitter, a craving for chocolate may mean that you need to eat more bitter foods such as green leafy vegetables. A desire for bitter foods or tart foods can also be a signal that the body needs help with digestion.

When it comes to chocolate, there is no doubt that you are also craving the added sugar, and must address this craving as well. A craving for sugar and other sweets can be a cry for overall nourishment. Sugar cravings may also indicate low blood sugar and a need for more protein or complex carbohydraes to stabilize it.

factoid: *Craving and overeating fatty foods, especially when you are trying not to, is a signal that something is wrong. The solution is not to cut out all fats, but to find the right fats.*

— Julia Ross, *The Diet Cure*

helpful herbs & whole food supplements

When used in combination with a nutrient-rich diet, certain herbs and whole food supplements can also help remedy food cravings and addictions.

Quality whole food supplements that contain an array of fruits and vegetables are at the top of my list for overall reduction and clearing of food cravings and addictions. They nourish the body at a cellular level and for many people quiet the body's demand for poor quality foods unlike anything else. As with all supplements, some people will need to consume them regularly for some time before they see results while others will notice results right away.

Green food supplements, when taken regularly, are especially helpful for staving off cravings by contributing to your overall nourishment. Barley grass in particular quells cravings for sweets because it helps balance blood sugar. In fact, it is recommended by the American Diabetic Association for just this reason. Taking an essential fatty acid supplement is also important especially if you crave fatty foods.

The closer a food is to its whole, fresh, natural state, the higher its nutritional value.

In the realm of herbs, oatstraw, cinnamon bark, dandelion, lemon balm, skullcap and bergamot are all helpful for cravings and addictions in general. As for specifics, bergamot is especially helpful for easing caffeine and salt addictions, and anything that balances blood sugar will help clear cravings for sweets such as fennel, fenugreek, coriander and dill. There are also herbal combinations available for sugar cravings, caffeine and tobacco withdrawal.

Herbs are readily available in bulk, capsule and tincture form at all health food stores. Whatever form of herbs you choose to use, experiment with small doses of one at a time to see what works best or consult with a knowledgeable herbalist. If you are taking medications, be sure to check for any adverse herbal or drug interactions before you begin.

Homeopathic remedies can also assist in clearing food cravings and addictions. You can do some research and experiment with this approach on your own as well. Try homeopathic combinations at the health food store for specific cravings such as caffeine to start. Because it is such a specialized modality, however, it is best to consult with a qualified homeopath for help if you can.

steer your thoughts

Finally, the general care of your body and mind are critical as well when trying to elude the clutches of cravings and addictions of any kind. Exercise, stress reduction and quality, supportive relationships can all help in this regard.

A helpful tip for overcoming your desire for certain foods in the psychological department is to stop thinking about them. When you find yourself thinking about how a particular food tastes— stop thinking about it! Just don't let your thoughts go there.

Some people advocate smelling a forbidden food or having just a little bite and either swallowing it or spitting it out. You can experiment to see if this works for you. I know a couple people who swear by it, but this has never worked for me. You wouldn't tell a heroine addict to just shoot up a little bit or just smell it, it would be all over. In my experience it is better to just not go there.

Thoughts of these foods and cravings for them will go away, but not if you keep indulging in them. So, whether it's on a billboard or T.V. commercial or worse yet, sitting right in front of you, don't let your mind indulge in thoughts of how good whatever it is you're looking at would taste. Instead, train yourself to ignore it. You will naturally begin to take your thoughts away from poor-quality addictive foods as your cravings and desire for them subsides. Making a little conscious effort to do so in the beginning will help things along.

Training yourself not to fantasize about bad foods is helpful. But training yourself not to actually *eat* them is essential. Whether it's stimulants, pseudofoods, or food allergens, if you don't eliminate foods that are offensive to your system for at least the time it takes to restore balance, you'll never get rid of the cravings for them, even if you're doing everything else right. Clearing the physical hold that unhealthy foods have on you is imperative to truly free yourself of them. Remember, your body craves what you feed it.

section three

Eating-for-Health Guideline #3:
Eat an Abundance of Whole, Fresh, Natural Foods

No-Nonsense Nutrition

Article Series ~ By Kelly Hayford, CNC, Author *If It's Not Food, Don't Eat It!*

Eating-for-Health Guideline #3:
Eat an Abundance of Whole, Fresh, Natural Foods

Simply stated, *Eating-for-Health Guideline #3* is:

eat an abundance of whole, fresh, natural foods
   …and little to no processed foods.

It seems easy enough, but experience has shown me that the majority of people today are confused about the terms *whole*, *fresh* and *natural* when it comes to what they eat. In our modern, urbanized culture most people are completely disconnected from the source of their food, which has resulted in a great lack of knowledge about what's going into their mouths.

The easiest way to know if a food is whole, fresh and natural is to ask if you could find it in nature. Would you see it in the jungle, in the forest or on a farm? Have you ever heard of a *Tator-Tot* tree or a bagel bush? If not, then it's processed. The following definitions are helpful for further clarification and inspiration

whole
Identifying a *whole* food is easy. Just think of any food that is completely intact just as Mother Nature made it. Any produce, such as apples, whole grains such as brown rice, vegetable proteins such as beans, and animal proteins such as eggs or fish. That's pretty much it, any food that contains *all* of its parts and nutrients. In contrast, food that has been ground, separated, processed, and stripped of its parts and valuable nutrients, would *not* be considered a *whole* food.

People often say they eat whole grains regularly because they buy whole wheat or whole grain bread. Certainly whole grain bread is a *better* choice and may be closer to whole than white bread, but don't be fooled into thinking you're eating whole grains. Bread is not a whole grain. It is bread. And bread is a processed food no matter how you slice it. It may be processed without chemical additives (check the label to be sure!), but it's processed nevertheless—i.e. ground, baked, mixed with other, sometimes mysterious and unpronounceable ingredients, etc.

fresh
If food has been cooked, processed or preserved in any way, it is not fresh. Of course there are degrees of freshness to consider as well. For example, produce trucked in from the farm to your local store is going to be less fresh than produce picked from your garden (which is as fresh as you can get!) but still much fresher than frozen, canned, or dried produce. The same may be said of meats, poultry and dairy products.

Mother Nature has an automatic expiration date system installed in her food products. It's called rotting! Something that doesn't ever rot or takes a very long time to rot would obviously not be considered fresh (with the exception of properly-stored grains or legumes which have a naturally long shelf life).

Section 3, No. 1

Copyright 2008
Kelly Hayford

The fresher food is, the more alive it is, which means the more enzymes and life-force energy it contains. Most Americans have a deficiency of vitamins, minerals, and enzymes because they do not eat a large enough variety and quantity of fresh, raw fruits and vegetables. This is the single biggest root-cause health issue in America today.

natural

The principle of *natural* is a little trickier and the topic of some debate, at least among the FDA and food manufacturers who have to adhere to agreed upon usage of the word natural when it comes to labeling. Getting into that topic could take up an entire volume. So to make it easy, for our purposes here, we will define natural foods as those that Mother Nature has provided us (as opposed to a manufacturer), are not refined or processed or minimally so, and do not contain any artificial or chemical additives, such as colorings, preservatives, flavor enhancers, etc.

As with each of the preceding definitions, there are degrees to which a food may be considered *natural*. For example, a store bought can of tomato sauce that *does not* contain any preservatives or chemical additives would be *more* natural than another brand that *does* contain preservatives and additives. While a fresh batch of tomatoes from the garden or produce section cooked down to tomato sauce would be more natural and fresher than either of the canned products.

Another important consideration on the topic of natural has to do with *how* we eat our food. Many people who advocate an all raw, or a predominately-raw foods diet believe that cooking food is not natural. On the other hand, fire is a natural element as well, and has been used to cook foods since humans lived in caves. I tend to agree with the more moderate position of including a combination of both raw and cooked foods in the diet. Most Americans could, however, benefit from eating *more* raw foods, as mentioned.

little to no processed foods

Whole, fresh, natural foods are completely intact, and contain all of their original enzymes, life-force energy, and nutrients, thus supporting, strengthening, and nourishing the body. Processed foods have lost many, and sometimes all of these vital elements. Consequently, not only do they not provide complete nourishment, they rob the body of nutrients through the effort of processing them. This renders them *anti-nutrients*, which deplete and degenerate the body and cause *dis*-ease.

Don't be misled by processed foods with labels saying 'enriched' or 'fortified.' The synthetic chemicals added to masquerade as vitamins and minerals are anything but natural, and do nothing for the devitalized food products to which they are added, as they are still devoid of most enzymes and fiber. In addition, most popular-brand processed foods on the market today contain toxic, chemical additives that further contribute to numerous symptoms and *dis*-eases in the body, alter the body's natural instincts and cause unnatural food cravings.

There is a vast difference between foods that have been processed with chemical additives and those that have not. Natural-brand processed foods can be a great transition or occasional item. But remember these are *still* processed foods and ideally kept to a minimum as well.

No-Nonsense Nutrition

Article Series ~ By Kelly Hayford, CNC, Author *If It's Not Food, Don't Eat It!*

Suggested Fruits & Vegetables
The Foundation of an Eating-for-Health Lifestyle

factoid: *In over 4500 research articles reviewed, fruits & vegetables came out as the #1 blocker in the reduction of the incidence of cancer.*

This and the next few articles will focus on suggested whole, fresh, natural foods for you to enjoy in abundance (barring any specific food allergies or sensitivities). For further assistance in getting to know natural foods, my favorite comprehensive resource is *The New Whole Foods Encyclopedia*, by Rebecca Wood. Entries include information on the origin of the food, its health benefits, uses, and practical tips on buying, storing and cooking.

Another great book for learning about produce in particular, is *The Field Guide to Produce*, by Aliza Green. It not only provides tips on choosing, storing and cooking specific items, but also features a convenient color photo index. It's also pocket-sized so you can bring it to the grocery store with you.

These are two books for the shelf of anyone who is serious about eating natural, healthy foods. For now, the following list and general descriptions will get you started.

fruits

Sweet, succulent, juicy, nectar of God is the best way to describe these marvels of nature. Both fresh and dried fruits are great to keep on hand to liven up a dish or as a stand- alone snack. Check the labels on dried fruit to be sure there are no additives such as sugar, colorings, or preservatives. If you run across dried fruits such as apricots, apples, and raisins that are light in color, they may have been treated with toxic sulfites. Dried fruits that are not treated will be brown and more shriveled by comparison. They may not look as pretty, but they are a much better choice health-wise.

apples	grapefruit	(oranges)
apricots	kiwi	papayas
(bananas)	lemons	peaches
(berries)	limes	pears
cherries	mangoes	pineapple
figs	melons	plums
grapes	nectarines	tangelos

non-starchy vegetables

Non-starchy vegetables are the only food that everyone seems to agree we should all be eating in abundance. At the same time they are, ironically, the one food that everyone is eating the *least*. This is true of Americans anyway. In many traditional cultures, vegetables are the mainstay of their diet, which, in large part, accounts for their comparatively lower incidence of chronic degenerative *dis*-ease. As a cul-

Section 3, No. 2

Copyright 2008
Kelly Hayford

ture, our eating habits have unfortunately strayed from these vital plant foods and we're paying the price. We must take a cue from traditional cultures and reacquaint ourselves with the regular preparation and consumption of vegetables. Begin by perusing this list. Upcoming articles contain tips for food shopping and preparation and will help you further in making these nutrient-packed foods part of your daily diet.

asparagus	cilantro	peas
(avocado)	collard greens	peppers
beans *(green & yellow)*	cucumber	radish
beets	(eggplant)	salad greens
beet greens	jicama	sea vegetables
bok choy	kale	(spinach)
broccoli	leeks	sprouts
cabbage	lettuce	swiss chard
carrots (raw)	mustard greens	(tomatoes)
cauliflower	mushrooms	watercress
celery	onions	zucchini

starchy vegetables

Starchy vegetables are a hearty, satisfying part of a natural, balanced diet. Because most are root vegetables, they are especially beneficial in the cold months due to their warming properties. They are also versatile. You can cook them whole, chop into bite-sized chunks, or purée for a rich sauce or soup base. Another nice feature is that most starchy vegetables have a relatively long shelf life when stored properly, making them easy and convenient to keep on hand.

artichokes	(potatoes)	sweet potatoes
burdock root *(cooked)*	pumpkins	turnips
carrots *(cooked)*	rutabagas	yams
parsnips	squash	

note: *Not all foods listed are going to be appropriate for everybody. Foods in parentheses indicate foods that may be problematic for some people. They are either common food allergens or difficult to digest. Make a mental note of these foods and take notice of any possible reactions to or difficulties you may have with them.*

No-Nonsense Nutrition

Article Series ~ By Kelly Hayford, CNC, Author *If It's Not Food, Don't Eat It!*

Section 3, No. 3

Copyright 2008
Kelly Hayford

Suggested Whole Grains

For thousands of years whole grains have been humanities most important food. They supply the body with almost every nutrient it needs. They're easy to grow, harvest, store and transport. In most parts of the world even today they provide one of the cheapest sources of nourishment.

In the U.S. and other Western nations, however, highly-processed white refined flour made into cereals, breads, pastries and snacks have overtaken nutrient– and fiber-rich whole grains. These often overly-sweetened pseudofoods are harmful to the body. The information here will help you get familiar with whole grains. If you get hungry for more, check out Rebecca Wood's book, *The Splendid Grain*.

gluten grains

Remember as a child mixing flour and water to make glue? It was the gluten contained in the flour that gave this mixture its sticky, glue-like consistency. Gluten is a mixture of gum-like, water-insoluble plant proteins found in many grains. Great stuff for binding paper maché, not so good for the intestines or any other part of the digestive and eliminative tract.

The following grains all contain various amounts of gluten, with wheat containing the most. This is the primary reason wheat is problematic for so many people. Many people who are allergic or sensitive to wheat have difficulty with other gluten grains as well and are better off eating the non-gluten grains that follow. Others do just fine with gluten grains other than wheat, however. Test different grains to see how you do. Spelt and kamut are the two grains closest in taste and texture to wheat. Because of their lower gluten content, however, they are often easier to tolerate.

barley	rye	(wheat)
kamut	spelt	
oats	tef	

non-gluten grains

Whether you have a pronounced sensitivity to gluten grains or not, it is wise to regularly partake of the non-gluten grains as well. You don't want to miss out on the nutrients and fiber they offer, and also the opportunity to give your system a break from having to deal with the thicker, stickier gluten grains.

Brown rice can sometimes be challenging for those who have weakened digestion or elimination. In which case, this otherwise beneficial gain should be avoided, at least temporarily until you are able to process it adequately. White basmati rice would be a better choice until your system is stronger as it is much easier to digest. Make sure it is basmati rice and not regular white or instant rice.

amaranth	brown rice	quinoa
buckwheat	(corn)	wild rice
basmati rice (brn/wht)	millet	

note: *Foods in parentheses are common food allergens or difficult to digest for some people.*

tips for cooking whole grains

The general protocol for cooking perfect grains every time is as follows:

- *place grain in sieve, remove any rocks or debris, and rinse in cold water*
- *combine grain with water and pinch of salt in appropriate-sized stainless steel or enameled pot*
- *bring grain and water to a boil uncovered*
- *reduce heat to low, stir, cover*
- *cook without stirring until all water is absorbed (time will depend on grain)*

The ratio of one part grain to two parts water works well for many grains, and is a good rule of thumb to use if you have forgotten the specifics for the grain you are cooking. Some grains require a little less water, while others require a little more. Because cooking time and water ratio vary depending on the variety of grain, it is best to write down instructions when buying grains from the bulk bins, or simply follow the instructions given if packaged. This chart is also helpful...

per cup	cups water	cooking time
amaranth	1 ¼	20 min.
barley	2 ½ - 3	40-60 min.
buckwheat	2	12 min.
basmati rice	1 ¾	15-20 min.
millet	2 – 2 ½	20-30 min.
oats (whole)	2	45 min.
quinoa	2	15-25 min.
rice *(short grain brown)*	1 ½ - 2	40 min.
rice *(long grain)*	2 – 2 ¼	45-60 min.
tef	1 ½	20 min.

more tips & tidbits

- *When cooking grains, keep heat on low to reduce scorching or sticking to the bottom of the pan. To loosen grain that has stuck to the bottom, remove pan from heat leaving the cover on for a couple of minutes. Then stir loosened grain up from the bottom. (Works only if grain hasn't been scorched.)*
- *For a nutty flavor, grains may be toasted alone or with a small amount of ghee or oil before adding water. Spices, fresh ginger or garlic are also a delightful addition.*
- *Substitute half or all of the water with chicken or vegetable broth for added flavor.*
- *For fast and easy whole grains, invest in a rice cooker. Just set it up with timer and leave it!*

product recommendation

Bob's Red Mill offers the best whole grain products on the market. They stone grind a variety of whole grains into flours and meals on over one-hundred-year-old mills, then mix them into an array of unique cereals, pancake and waffle mixes, bread mixes, gluten free mixes, and specialty products. They make it easy to have these fiber-rich foods a regular part of your diet.

No-Nonsense Nutrition

Article Series ~ By Kelly Hayford, CNC, Author *If It's Not Food, Don't Eat It!*

Section 3, No. 4

Copyright 2008
Kelly Hayford

Suggested Fats, Oils, Nuts & Seeds

factoid: *Polynesian islanders, who get most of their fat calories from coconut oil have an exceedingly low rate of heart disease. Coconut oil is less likely than other oils to cause obesity, because the body easily converts it into energy rather than depositing its calories as body fat.*

—Linda Page, N.D., *Healthy Healing*

The low-fat fad has made many people fat-phobic. This is unfortunate as fats are highly beneficial to the body—the *good* fats, that is. The good fats provide essential fatty acids that nourish the brain, lubricate internal tissues and organs, assist digestion and elimination, and take part in hormone production—to name just a few. They're absence in the American diet is one of the primary causes of symptoms and *dis*-ease. So fear fats no more! Familiarize yourself with the suggested fats, oils, nuts and seeds listed here. If you have been on a low-fat or no-fat diet go easy to start to allow your system time to adjust.

oils

Look for oils that are unrefined, cold-pressed, and virgin or extra virgin whenever possible. Heat alters the nature of oils and renders them harmful to the body. Cold pressing oils prevents damage to the essential fats caused by the heat process, thereby, maintaining the beneficial nature of the oil. Virgin and extra-virgin is the highest quality oil, as it has been extracted from the best produce of the harvest from the first pressing. Following is a list of recommended oils:

(butter) or ghee (clarified butter)
coconut oil
hemp oil
olive oil (extra virgin)

(flaxseed oil) - do not heat!
sesame seed oil
sunflower oil

Contrary to what we have been told the last couple of decades, coconut oil is the best all-around oil to keep on hand. It is the only oil that maintains its integrity when heated and offers a long list of healthful benefits. It's also delicious!

In Thailand people use coconut oil and drink coconut milk with the same frequency that we drink cow's milk in this country, and have comparatively low rates of obesity, heart disease, and osteoporosis. They're obviously doing something right and we could take some pointers. For more on the health benefits, *The Coconut Oil Miracle*, by Bruce Fife, is a great read and also explains the politics behind why this highly beneficial oil was falsely vilified in recent years.

Choose from virgin coconut oil, which has a full-bodied coconut taste that adds a satisfying richness to everything you make with it. My favorite brand is made by *Jungle Products*. For dishes you'd rather *not* have taste like coconut or if you don't like the taste of coconut, try expeller-pressed which is slightly more processed yielding a much milder taste than virgin coconut oil.

Extra virgin olive oil is the next best all-around oil to keep around and is especially nice for salads and dipping. Butter is also a nice condiment and in addition to coconut oil, is the best choice for baking. Unrefined sesame oil maintains its integrity at medium temperatures and, consequently, is a good choice for low-heat stir-frying. When sautéing vegetables or meats, use a small amount of olive or sesame oil with a little bit of water and keep temperature below 350°. Use coconut oil if you want to turn the heat up on a stir fry, for example. It is the only oil that maintains its integrity at high temperatures.

Margarine is not recommended for any use as it contains hydrogenated oils. There are also a few spreads on the market today made from a blend of oils and ingredients. Although these are often *thought* to be a healthy choice, they're highly processed and often loaded with additives. Similarly, canola oil is another highly-processed, toxic oil. Unfortunately, due to media hype it has made its way into many natural brand products because it is cheap and many people are misinformed.

factoid: *In 1900, heart disease accounted for 8% of deaths in America. Almost 80% of fat consumed at that time came from animal sources such as lard and butter, as well as coconut oil. Over the century man-made fats such as margarine and vegetable shortening increased as the state of our health decreased. By 1950, heart disease was the #1 cause of death and remains so at 40% today.*

nuts & seeds

Avoid roasted, salted nuts and seeds, especially pseudofood brands that contain additives such as dyes or MSG. Instead, choose raw, unsalted nuts and seeds in their natural state or *crispy nuts* (see below), as they provide a good source of healthy fats. Limit daily consumption of nuts and seeds to 1-2 small handfuls per day (approximately ⅛-¼ cup). Any more than this can be challenging to digest. If you have known, or suspected problems with your liver or gallbladder, irritable bowl or a generally weakened digestive system, do not eat any nuts or seeds initially. When your digestion is stronger, try introducing a few soaked almonds (see below) and see how you do.

Contrary to popular belief, cashews are beans and peanuts are legumes. Both are common allergens so it's wise to test for any sensitivity. When it comes to nut butters, buy all natural brands that don't contain sugar, emulsifiers or other additives. Stir the oil that floats to the top in with the butter with a knife and keep in the fridge to keep fresh. Peanut and almond butter ground on site are your best choices. Of the two, almond butter is better all-around because it contains less fat, is much easier to digest, and tastes delicious. Tahini, or sesame seed butter, is another good choice.

almonds & almond butter	pecans
(cashews)	pumpkin seeds
flax seeds (ground)	sesame seeds & tahini (sesame seed butter)
hemp seeds	sunflower seeds
(peanuts & peanut butter)	walnuts

tips & tidbits

- *Try chopped hemp seeds on whole-grain toast with butter or hemp oil for a delicious dose of good fats.*

- *Soak raw almonds in water overnight for easier digestion. Rinse and slide off skins in the morning. Keep refrigerated to preserve freshness.*

- *To make nuts even easier to digest, soak overnight in water 2-3" inches above the nuts and 1 tsp sea salt. Drain in morning, spread on cookie sheets and dry in oven on lowest heat setting for 12-24 hours. Cool and store these "crispy nuts" in fridge.*

(note: Foods in parentheses are either common food allergens or difficult to digest for some people.)

Suggested Meats, Fish, Poultry & Beans

to eat or not to eat—meat?

Probably the most hotly contested debate regarding the human diet is that of the meat-eaters versus the vegetarians. As with any issue that seems to be extremely polarized, myself and many others tend to believe that the truth lies somewhere in the middle.

The most important thing is that you discover what is right for your body at this time in your life and be honest with yourself about whether or not something is working for you. Take into consideration that Americans in general eat *way* too much animal protein. Most Americans are eating animal protein 2-3 times *a day*, which is excessive. Cutting animal protein consumption down to 3-5 times a week (including dairy products, provided you can tolerate them) is a much healthier range.

Also take into consideration that being a vegetarian does not mean you have a healthy diet. In fact, many vegetarians have very poor diets. Not knowing any better, what many vegetarians do, as I did myself when I was a vegetarian, is abstain from animal protein and eat lots of simple carbohydrates. If you are going to be a vegetarian remember that the definition of vegetarian is someone who eats lots and lots of *vegetables*. Adhere to this true definition and you'll be better off.

animal protein

Many non-vegetarian pioneers of the health food movement, such as Dr. Bernard Jensen, recommend having animal protein 3-5 times a week. Give or take a serving, this is generally accepted as an adequate amount to satisfy the body's nutritional needs, while at the same time not too much to risk clogging your system.

Fresh free-range and grass-fed organic animal protein free of additives, hormones, pesticides and antibiotics is always your first choice whenever available. Meat packers that offer these quality standards boldly display this on their tags and labels. If you do not see this information displayed anywhere, you can be sure that one or more of these harmful substances is present and better left alone. When preparing animal protein it is best to cook at lower heats for longer times. In other words, bake, broil, grill, or roast it to preserve the integrity and nutritional value.

beef	fish
bison	lamb
chicken	ostrich
(eggs)	wild game

(dairy products)

Once again, if you are going to indulge in dairy products, be sure to choose organic products free of preservatives, hormones, pesticides and antibiotics. Fresh from the farm, raw, unpasteurized is best. The pasteurization process uses heat that alters the nature of the milk protein and renders it harmful to the body. Raw milk and dairy products are available in retail stores and farmer's markets in some states. In others, you can get them straight from the farm by buying a share in a cow. This is also a great way to get organic, grass-fed meats. For farms that offer this service in your area, go to: www. RealMilk.com.

Also check labels to be sure you are getting *real* cheese, butter, and yogurt that do not contain additives, artificial sweeteners or refined sugars. Fake-food dairy products that say 'lite', for example often contain these toxic substances.

Keep in mind that dairy foods are at the top of the list of common food allergens and as a result, may need to be completely eliminated from or included only on a rotational basis in many people's diets. Even if you do not have a known or pronounced problem with dairy—unless it is the highest-quality (i.e. raw, unpasteurized from grass-fed, pastured cows)—it is a food to limit in your diet for reasons to be discussed in an upcoming article.

(butter)	(kefir)	(yogurt)
(cheese)	(milk)	

beans & vegetable protein

Beans are a nutrient-dense food savored throughout the world for their economical, life-sustaining properties. Beans are a great food to include in your regular menu planning, especially if you are looking to cut down on the amount of animal protein in your diet and save money at the same time. Cook up a batch of spicy or seasoned beans and rice, add a side of mixed veggies, and you've got a satisfying meal for pennies. Keep additive-free canned beans on hand for a quick and easy alternative.

As we are all aware however, beans are the musical fruit. Which means, they can be difficult for many people to digest. If this is the case, you should limit them to 1-2 servings a week, or leave them alone completely until your digestion is stronger and better able to tolerate them. Remember, any food is only highly beneficial to you if YOU can digest it and it agrees with YOUR system.

Soaking beans over night will reduce their cooking time and reduce the flatulence production factor as well. Adding a piece of kombu seaweed to the pot while cooking can also reduce gas production, as it helps to break down the hard outer shell of the bean and consequently, increases digestibility. Some beans are easier to digest than others. Experiment to find which are best for you.

If you can tolerate soy, soy-based products such as tofu and tempeh are another great source of plant-based protein. Be sure to get those made from non-GMO soy.

adzuki beans	lentils	(tempeh -soy)
beans & bean sprouts	(miso)	(tofu - soy)
kidney beans	mung beans	white beans

note: *Foods in parentheses are either common food allergens or difficult to digest for some people.*

No-Nonsense Nutrition

Article Series ~ By Kelly Hayford, CNC, Author *If It's Not Food, Don't Eat It!*

Natural Sweeteners

Virtually everybody has an issue with sugar in one form or another these days as evidenced by the growing diabetes epidemic and skyrocketing number of those with pre-diabetes and other sugar-related conditions.

As with other foods, there is a wide spectrum of sweeteners. At one end of the spectrum would be white-refined sugar and high-fructose corn syrup, probably the two that cause the most harm to the body. On the other end of the spectrum is *stevia*, which is actually beneficial to the body and has little to no effect on the blood sugar. Concentrated sweeteners of any kind, natural or otherwise, are best kept to a minimum. Consider foods made with them as special treats rather than daily events.

When you do indulge, the natural sweeteners that follow are your best choice. On a regular basis, keep them to a minimum in accordance with your tolerance level. And cut them out completely if you are experiencing any *dis*-ease, especially low-ered immune function or lack of energy.

agave	date sugar	stevia
barley malt	raw honey	rapadura
brown rice syrup	maple syrup	sucanat
pure fruit juice, jam	molasses	

limit *all* sweets to occasional treats

A woman once came to me because every winter she would get recurrent colds and upper respiratory infections that would linger on for weeks at a time. She was puzzled and frustrated as to why this was happening because relative to the average American, she maintained a pretty wholesome diet, eating fruits and vegetables and all organic foods regularly. When I looked at her food diary, how-ever, her problem became clear.

She ate a substantial amount of sweets with almost reckless abandon. Because they were homemade with natural sweeteners such as maple syrup and honey, she mistakenly thought it wasn't a problem. As soon as she reduced the amount of sweets she was eating, her health and energy improved.

Like this client, people often mistakenly believe that natural sweeteners are 'good' for you and don't have any ill effects when, in fact, while natural sweeteners such as those listed are a much better choice than refined sugars, they are still extreme foods that have a stimulating effect and with regular or over consumption can cause the same problems as refined sugars.

quote: *I am fond of telling people that if something tastes sweet you probably should spit it out as it is not likely to be too good for you. This of course, is a humorous exaggeration, but for most people who struggle with chronic illness, it is likely to be a helpful guide.*

— Dr. Joseph Mercola

Section 3, No. 6

Copyright 2008
Kelly Hayford

stevia: the natural herbal sweetener

Stevia is a natural herbal sweetener that is 200-300 times sweeter than sugar. In contrast to sugar, however, it actually has medicinal properties that are beneficial to the body. For this and other reasons listed below, stevia is your best choice when it comes to a concentrated sweetener.

things to know about stevia

1 ~ Stevia is a natural herbal sweetener that actually helps regulate blood sugar.

2 ~ Stevia is great for diabetics, hypoglycemics and anyone trying to kick the sugar habit.

3 ~ Stevia is a wonderful aid to anyone trying to lose weight as it has no calories and, when consumed regularly, reduces cravings for sweet and fatty foods.

4 ~ Stevia also lowers elevated blood pressure, boosts the immune system, improves digestion and is beneficial to the skin.

5 ~ Stevia products vary widely, so if you have tried one and didn't like it—try another brand! (There are a couple that are a bit nasty, quite honestly.)

6 ~ Stevia can be found in the supplement section of the natural foods stores, purchased online or from direct distributors.

7 ~ My favorite brands are available from the *Young Living* and the *Sunrider* companies, as well as *Stevia Glycerite* by NOW, available at health food stores.

8 ~ *Stevia Rebaudiana: Nature's Sweet Secret*, by David Richard contains more great information about stevia, its benefits and its history.

9 ~ *If It's Not Food, Don't Eat It!*, by Kelly Hayford and *Stevia: Naturally Sweet Recipes for Desserts, Drinks, and More*, by Rita Depuydt both contain recipes using stevia.

note: *Keep in mind that even "the best" sweetener perpetuates the taste for sweets and should be considered a transitional food item that eventually becomes an occasional treat, if you really want to overcome cravings and break a sugar addiction.*

recommended product

Stevia is available in three primary forms: crushed green leaves and powder (the most natural), white powder and as a liquid herbal extract. Some of the extracts are preserved in a small amount of alcohol. This evaporates out when baked or added to tea, so you will not taste it.

Stevia Glycerite by NOW is one of my favorite stevia products. Unlike many others, it doesn't have a strong after taste and it's alcohol-free. Try different brands and forms to discover what works best for you.

Suggested Herbs, Spices & Dressings

old proverb: *If they would drink nettles in March and eat mugwort in May, so many fine maidens wouldn't go to the clay.*

herbs & spices

Travel around the world and you will have dishes placed before you brimming with both common and exotic herbs and spices. Scout around most American kitchens however, and you'll be hard-pressed to find anything other than the classic salt and pepper shaker strategically placed on the dining table. If you do find a spice rack, it was most likely acquired as a Christmas gift and is now collecting dust or never been opened. This is a shame because these marvelous gifts of nature don't just add flavor, they are packed with nutrients and offer a wide variety of therapeutic properties as well.

In addition to a host of individual properties, herbs and spices are powerful immune boosters that keep the body healthy and strong. Probably the most important feature that almost all herbs and spices offer is that they help with the digestion and elimination of food. When you deprive yourself of herbs and spices, you are also depriving yourself of the therapeutic benefits they have to offer.

So, next time you're cooking try spicing things up a bit. Adding herbs and spices into your diet in cooked foods, fresh salads, or drinking herbal teas is a really easy and enjoyable way to upgrade the quality of your diet. It is particularly smart to add in those that are known to aid any specific symptoms or *dis*-eases you may be experiencing. Following is just a partial list of suggested herbs and spices:

anise	dill	pepper
basil	fennel	peppermint
bay leaf	garlic	rosemary
cardamom	ginger	saffron
cayenne	lemongrass	sage
cinnamon	marjoram	spearmint
clove	oregano	tarragon
coriander	nutmeg	thyme
cumin	parsley	turmeric

Also, take advantage of the fabulous herb and spice blends, liquid flavorings and don't forget salt—the *good* salt that is (i.e. unrefined, additive-free *real* salt). Here's some you'll find in my kitchen:

Bragg's Sprinkle	(Bragg's Liquid Aminos)
Herbamare	(tamari sauce)
Tocomere	(soy sauce)
Mrs. Dash	Gomasio
(Spike)	Redmond's Sea Salt
Trader Joe's 21-Seasoning Salute	Himalayan pink salt

note: *Foods in parentheses are either common food allergens, contain common food allergens, or may otherwise be problematic for some people.*

No-Nonsense Nutrition

Article Series ~ By Kelly Hayford, CNC, Author *If It's Not Food, Don't Eat It!*

condiments & dressings

Similarly, when it comes to dressings and condiments most American kitchens are equipped with the standard fake-food brand ketchup, mustard, bottled dressings, and little else. My kitchen is stocked with these cultural standards as well; the natural, additive-free varieties, of course! Here's a few you may want to keep on hand:

> Spectrum Naturals Olive Oil Mayonaise
> Westbrae Ketchup
> Westbrae Mustard
> Bragg's Salad Dressings w/olive oil
> Annie's Naturals Salad Dressings
> Seeds of Change Salad Dressings

You can also easily make up your own blend of herbs and spices, or homemade dressings. You can drizzle a combination of olive or flax oil and lemon or balsamic vinegar over steamed vegetables or a fresh salad (remember not to heat flax oil). Or marinate chopped vegetables in olive oil and lemon juice or balsamic vinegar before roasting or grilling.

favorite dressing & marinade recipe

I keep the following ingredients on hand at all times. I use them in different combinations for salad dressing and marinating vegetables, chicken and fish before grilling. Most everybody likes this combination:

> Fresh lemon juice or balsamic vinegar
> Extra virgin olive oil
> Bragg's liquid aminos
> Spike, Sprinkle or Trader Joe's 21-Seasoning Salute

Keeping these items on hand makes flavoring foods simple and healthy. I personally never measure it out. I simply drizzle on the olive oil, then drizzle on a little less lemon juice or balsamic vinegar, give it a few sprays of Bragg's (see below) and a few shakes of seasoning and toss. Experiment to find the amounts that appeal to you. You can start by measuring the standard 1 part acid, in this case lemon juice or vinegar, to 2 parts of the olive oil.

recommended product

Bragg Liquid Aminos is similar to soy sauce or tamari. It's liquid protein concentrate that contains an array of important healthy amino acids. Made from non-GMO soybeans and purified water, it's not fermented or heated and gluten free. It's great on virtually everything and virtually everyone seems to like it.

I recommend you get the smaller spray bottle to start. Then buy the larger bottle and refill as necessary. It is very concentrated, so a little bit goes a long way. Bragg's also offers high-quality olive oil, bottled dressings made with olive oil, apple cider vinegar and an all-purpose seasoning called *Sprinkle*. Give them all a try!

No-N☉nsense Nutrition

Article Series ~ By Kelly Hayford, CNC, Author *If It's Not Food, Don't Eat It!*

Whole Food Supplements
An Essential Part of Today's Healthy Diet

factoid: *You have to eat 6 apples today to get the same amount of nutrients our grandparent's would have gotten from just eating one.*

I highly recommend *everyone* consume whole food supplements daily. Why? Because most people eat mostly processed foods and the few whole, fresh, natural foods they do eat are depleted of enzymes and nutrients due to depleted soils from modern farming practices. There is no substitute for eating a healthy diet. However, whole food supplements are imperative for restoring and maintaining vital health and energy, as well as preventing future *dis*-ease.

Whole food supplements, as the name implies, are made of concentrated foods with all of their synergistic nutrients intact according to nature's original design. Quality whole food supplements are bio-available, nourish the cells, and do not cause nutritional imbalance or toxicity as isolated vitamins often do. They're available in convenient powder, capsule, and tablet form to suit individual needs.

How do you know if a product is a whole food supplement? Read the ingredients label. It will read like a grocery list (i.e., carrots, beets, spinach, kelp, broccoli, barley grass, etc.) rather than a list of isolated vitamins that have been extracted from food and isolated from their companion nutrients (i.e., Vitamin A, B, C, and so on). For those who are interested in learning more, *Man Cannot Live on Vitamins Alone*, by Dr. Vic Shayne is a great resource.

There are a variety of whole food supplements available today. Avoid those that contain common food allergens, herbs, or mix fruits and vegetables together. As with any food, not every whole food supplement is going to be right for every body. Not every whole food supplement is created equal either. Refer to the next article for tips on how to choose the best product for you.

Whole food supplements are especially helpful when it comes to meeting our daily quota of critically important dark green vegetables and essential fatty acids—the two most missing elements in our modern diets. At the *very least* everyone, especially children should be taking both. Ideally everyone should also be taking a fruit blend because virtually nobody is eating enough fruits or enough variety of fruits either.

green food supplements

Everyone agrees that eating fresh green vegetables regularly is paramount to optimal health. But how many of us actually do it? Whole food supplements derived from the fresh juices of wheat grass, barley grass, kamut, alfalfa, etc., or *green foods* as I call them, are a convenient, palatable way to incorporate these vital foods into your diet on a regular basis.

Like whole food supplements in general, there are a variety of green food supplements on the market today. They are available as individual green foods, such as

Section 3, No. 8

Copyright 2008
Kelly Hayford

alfalfa or wheat grass, and are also available in blends. Generally speaking, it is best to consume a green food blend regularly in order to provide the body with a wide array of healthful nutrients.

Green foods are great to have on hand as a quick remedy for almost anything, especially headaches, stomach upset, fatigue, imbalanced blood sugar, and more. Instead of reaching for over-the-counter drugs that have toxic side effects, reach for a dose of green foods and feel better naturally.

essential fatty acid supplements

Anyone eating our modern Western diet is not getting enough of the good fats and the essential fatty acids they provide. To top it off, the trans fats and hydrogenated oils, or the *bad* fats, that everyone is consuming too much of, actually deplete the body of the small amount, if any, of the good fats people are getting. For this reason, in addition to including the beneficial fats and oils in your diet, it is also important to be taking an essential fatty acid supplement daily.

As with green foods and whole food supplements in general, it is especially important for children to be getting these essential nutrients because their diets are so erratic and often even more deficient. One of the primary causes of ADD, ADHD, learning disabilities and behavioral problems is the lack of essential fatty acids necessary for proper brain function. The one I like most for both children and adults is *Cod Liver Oil*. It is available in liquid to take by the spoonful or gel caps which make it go down a lot easier. *Evening Primrose Oil* is another one I recommend for all women, especially those experiencing hormonal issues.

benefits of green foods & essential fatty acids:

Here are just a few of the benefits of consuming green foods and essential fatty acids regularly...

- *increase your energy and endurance*
- *improve digestion and eliminate constipation*
- *increase mental focus and clarity, reduced ADD, ADHD & learning disabilities*
- *balance hormones reducing headaches, cramping, hot flashes, etc.*
- *help clear acne and other skin problems*
- *prevent and help reverse cancer, arthritis, asthma, and other degenerative dis-eases*
- *balance blood sugar - great for diabetes, hyper- or hypoglycemia*
- *eliminate body odor and bad breath.*
- *boost the immune system - reducing colds, flu, allergies, hay fever, sinusitis, etc*
- *strengthen nails and hair*
- *reduce food cravings and sensitivities*
- *acts as a natural sunscreen when consumed regularly*
- *high in bio-available calcium to help prevent and reverse osteoporosis*
- *great for keeping pets healthy too!*

note: Take half the recommended dosage when first starting on whole food supplements, especially if you are sensitive or have never taken them before. Some people may initially experience classic detoxification symptoms such as fatigue, headache, runny nose, diarrhea, etc. This reaction is part of the body's natural cleansing process. If this does occur, cut back and gradually increase the dose over a couple of weeks. Soon you'll feel even better than before!

No-Nonsense Nutrition

Article Series ~ By Kelly Hayford, CNC, Author If It's Not Food, Don't Eat It!

Section 3, No. 9

Copyright 2008
Kelly Hayford

How to Choose a
Whole Food Supplement

factoid: *Research shows you have only a 2.5% chance of selecting a nutritional product in the market place that is both nontoxic and effective.*

-- Journal of the American Nutraceutical Association, Winter 1999

If you're planning on taking a whole food supplement every day and spending good money to do so, you'll want to be sure that what you're taking is safe and effective. To help you make a wise decision review the ingredients list first, write down any questions you may have and then call the company or speak to one of its representatives to find out information not contained on the label. Following are favorable things you'll want to look for and things you'll want to avoid.

things to look for...

reputable company
As with natural food brands it's best to go with well-established companies that have a long-held reputation for producing safe, effective products and operating with integrity.

synergistic ingredients
Look for ingredients that follow basic food combining principles. For example, fruits and vegetables should be separate and taken separately as well. The ingredients should also work together to provide maximum bioavailability and the most health benefits. Request information from the company about the synergistic nature and bioavailability of its formula.

quality control & processing
Be sure the company uses low heat when processing as heat destroys beneficial enzymes and nutrients. Produce should be mature or vine-ripened to ensure the highest nutrient content and the end product should be free of any toxins or contaminants such as yeast, mold, bacteria, pesticide or herbicide residue.

independent research
The only way to know for sure if a product is effective is by research done on that specific product. Look for the gold standard—i.e. independent research conducted by reputable institutions that is randomized, double-blind, placebo controlled, reproducible and published in peer-reviewed scientific journals.

things to avoid...

possible false claims
Beware of companies that lead with wildly miraculous claims about their products. If a product has independent research behind it, testimonials are unnecessary as the science speaks for itself.

lack of synergy & improper food combinations

It has become very popular to throw a whole bunch of ingredients in one formula or super powder, mixing fruits, vegetables, and legumes all together. To the unaware, this may seem like a great idea. However, what it really demonstrates is a lack of synergy and the basic principles of proper food combining. Would you sit down and eat a bowl full of fruits and vegetables and beans mixed together? No, of course not. Not only would it be unpalatable, but doing so can cause a host of digestive disturbances and lead to malabsorption of the nutrients contained in the foods and other problems. The same is true of whole food supplements that contain a mish-mash of incompatible ingredients.

common food allergens

Even if you think you don't have any food allergies or sensitivities, any common food allergens should not be taken on a daily basis to avoid developing a sensitivity to them. Best to go with a product that is allergen-free (see *Section 4* for more on food allergies and sensitivities).

stimulating or medicinal herbs

Whole food supplements that contain herbs should be avoided for several reasons. Herbs have medicinal properties and should only be taken in concentrated amounts on a daily basis when treating specific health conditions. Some herbs can actually become toxic to the system when taken daily over a long period of time. Similarly, a particular herb contained within a product if not appropriate may actually exacerbate a particular condition. Some companies add stimulating herbs to make you "feel good" when you take them. These stimulating herbs may tax your adrenals when taken long term.

There is also the risk of counter indications or adverse interactions with pharmaceutical drugs or even other herbal formulas you might be taking. For example, Saint-John's-Wort, which has been shown to help treat depression, is also known to reduce the effectiveness of some HIV and cardiovascular medications.

irrelevant or questionable research

Make sure the research being presented is primary research conducted on the specific whole food supplement itself, not on apples in general, for example. Just because apples provide certain benefits, doesn't mean that the whole food supplement end product provides those same benefits. Also be sure the research was undertaken by an independent, reputable institution, not by the company or affiliated organization.

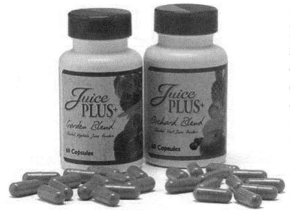

product recommendation

I have investigated and tried *many* different whole food supplements over the years. In terms of ingredients, *Juice Plus+®* is the only one I've found that I feel confidant about recommending to *everybody*. It doesn't contain anything allergenic, synthetic, or controversial and the formulas are synergistically combined. Most importantly, it is also the only product that has the depth and breadth of independent research behind it vouching for its safety and effectiveness. To learn more, visit: www.juiceplus.com.

No-Nonsense Nutrition

Article Series ~ By Kelly Hayford, CNC, Author *If It's Not Food, Don't Eat It!*

The Power of Fruits & Vegetables

From vegan to carnivore to low fat to high carb, the debate goes on about what is the best overall diet. In the midst of all the controversy however, there is one thing on which *everyone* agrees: *eat an abundant variety of fruits and vegetables.* In fact, the latest dietary guidelines recommend 5-13 servings of fruits and vegetables a day, depending on one's caloric intake. For a person who needs 2,000 calories a day, this translates into nine servings, or 4½ cups per day.

Although everyone agrees that fruits and vegetables are what we *should* be consuming the most, they are unfortunately what we are eating the least. Less than 10% of Americans are estimated to even come close to this recommendation.

The body craves what you feed it. So start feeding your body more fruits and vegetables and watch your desire for them grow. Start with your favorites and expand your selections from there.

research says!...

More and more research is emerging that supports the age-old notion that fruits and vegetables provide the greatest health benefits. Following are just a few examples to inspire you to make these health– and energy-giving foods the biggest part of your diet:

New research indicates that apples may improve memory and learning and protect the brain against oxidative damage that contributes to age-related disorders such as Alzheimer's disease. *-- Dr. Thomas Shea, University of Massachusetts*

Cranberries have many proven health benefits. They are high in antioxidants, cut bad cholesterol, raise good cholesterol, fight infection, prevent plaque formation on teeth, kill H. pylori bacteria, and more. *-- Amy Howell, Rutgers University*

In the Iowa Women's Health Study, women who ate the most green leafy vegetables were found to have less than half (44%) of the risk of ovarian cancer compared with subjects who ate the least. *-- The American Institute for Cancer Research*

In an international study, investigators found that people who ate plenty of fruits, vegetables and unsaturated fats but passed on sugary confections were less prone to wrinkling. *-- Journal of the American College of Nutrition*

Prostate cancer risk was cut by 41% among men who ate three or more servings of cruciferous vegetables (i.e. broccoli, cabbage, cauliflower, etc.) per week compared to those who ate less than one serving per week. *-- American Cancer Society*

Grape skin extracts (resveratrol) was able to inhibit the initiation and promotion of tumors, and cause pre-cancerous cells to return to normal.
-- *Science Journal, Jan, 1997*

Half cup of spinach 1x week reduces the incidence of macular degeneration and blindness by 33%.
-- *Massachusetts Eye & Ear Hospital*

According to a new joint study blueberries lessened pre-cancerous lesions in the colon by 57%. Another recent study shows that blueberries, particularly their skins, can also lower cholesterol.
-- *Rutgers University & the USDA*

A high consumption of fruits and vegetables is associated with a decreased risk of chronic diseases.
-- *Journal of Nutrition, 2000*

Green barley juice contains 13 times more carotene than carrots, 55 times more Vitamin C than apples, and 5 times more Iron than spinach!
-- *University of California, Davis*

A recent University of Illinois study on prostate cancer found that the phytochemical lycopene decreased tumor weights by 7-18%, while consuming broccoli and tomatoes together decreased tumor weights by a whopping 52%.
-- *Cancer Research Journal*

Evidence collectively demonstrates that fruit and vegetable intake is associated with improved health, reduced risk of major diseases, and possibly delayed onset of age related indicators.
-- *Diane Hyson, Ph.D., M.S., R.D.*

A study found those who ate cabbage and sauerkraut more than 3x a week were 72% less likely to develop breast cancer than those who had 1.5 or fewer servings.
-- *Michigan State University*

Eating plenty of fruits and vegetables can help you ward off heart disease and stroke, control blood pressure and cholesterol, prevent some types of cancer, avoid diverticultis, guard against cataract and macular degeneration, and more.
-- *Harvard School of Public Health*

Eating fruits and vegetables, particularly dark green leafy vegetables, appears to have a protective effect against coronary heart disease.
-- *Annals of Internal Medicine, June, 2001*

France's National Institute of Health & Medical Research found consuming large amounts and varieties of fruits, vegetables and whole-grain products daily may help prevent breast cancer.
-- *Journal of the National Cancer Institute*

People whose diets were high in fruits and vegetables were shown to have lower rates of angina, arthritis, asthma, bronchitis, cirrhosis, gallstones, heart attack, kidney stones, and peptic ulcers.
-- *Epidemiology, March 1998*

conclusion

You're grandmother was right: *eat your fruits and vegetables*. They're so good for you they can help save your life!

There isn't any condition in the body that can't be improved by improving your diet!

No-Nonsense Nutrition

Article Series ~ By Kelly Hayford, CNC, Author *If It's Not Food, Don't Eat It!*

Section 3, No. 11

Copyright 2008
Kelly Hayford

What About Organic?

This is a question I get asked often: *what do you think about organic?* Or, *do you think people should eat only organic?* Contrary to popular belief, there isn't a black and white answer to these questions. Instead, there are many variables to consider.

Twenty years ago if a product was labeled "organic" you could pretty much trust that it was, primarily because it wasn't the most popular farming method and in many cases wasn't profitable either. This just isn't true today. As the distrust of conventional methods of agribusiness has grown, organic products have become increasingly popular and in demand. Consequently, the whole business of organic has become increasingly confusing as a result.

Prior to any discussion about organic foods, it's important to understand what the official term "organic" means as it applies to our modern food supply. Here in the U.S., as of October 2002, all agricultural farms and products claiming to be organic must be guaranteed by a USDA-approved independent agency to be meeting the following guidelines:

- *Abstain from the application of prohibited materials (including synthetic fertilizers, pesticides, and sewage sludge) for 3 years prior to certification and then continually throughout their organic license.*

- *Prohibit the use of genetically modified organisms (GMO's) and irradiation.*

- *Employ positive soil building, conservation, manure management and crop rotation practices.*

- *Provide outdoor access and pasture for livestock. Refrain from antibiotic and hormone use in animals and sustain animals on 100% organic feed.*

- *Avoid contamination during the processing of organic products and keep records of all operations.*

I have often heard people refer to natural brand processed foods as being organic foods, or that Whole Foods or other health food stores, for example, sell only organic foods. This is *not* the case. While many of the natural brand processed foods are made with some or all organic ingredients, many of them are not.

Similarly, food products labeled "non-GMO," "free-range," or "hormone-free," aren't necessarily organic. Products can only be labeled organic, if they're grown and processed according to the USDA organic standards as described above.

organic vs. whole, fresh & natural

I know many well-educated individuals that go to great lengths and often great expense to be sure they're eating foods that are only labeled organic. They mistakenly believe that this is the most important factor when it comes to food choices. I can assure you, it is not!

A perfect illustration of this is a client I once worked with who bragged that for the previous 16 years she had eaten only organic foods. She was at least 120 pounds overweight and had multiple health conditions. She attributed these issues to a thyroid condition and genetics and she wanted me to help her get them under control with natural remedies and supplements. In fact, she initially refused to fill out a food diary because she insisted that her health problems weren't related to her diet because she ate only organic.

A review of her food diary when I finally received it, showed just what I suspected. She did in fact eat only food products that were labeled organic. Most of them however, were highly processed and contained high amounts of sugar, refined flour, salt and poor quality fats. She ate a lot of what I call organic junk food. As a friend of mine so aptly puts it, "Just because it's organic doesn't mean it's good for you!"

In addition, she ate very little whole, fresh, natural foods. Because fresh organic produce was hard to come by in her area, when she did eat fruits and vegetables they were usually frozen and sometimes canned. She rarely made brown rice or other whole grains, opting instead for refined carbohydrates such as pastas and breads made from organic grains.

As you are hopefully learning by now, it was no surprise that as this client began to reduce her intake of organic *processed* foods and increase the amount of whole, fresh, natural foods, whether they were organic or not, her weight began to go down and her health began to improve.

is it more nutritious?

Under the ideal conditions of strictly controlled research, more and more studies reveal that organic tomatoes, corn, and some other fruits and vegetables contain more nutrients, especially antioxidants. Under real world conditions however, conditions vary from farm to farm and field to field.

Whether or not any given piece of produce is more nutritious than another will depend on where it was grown, it's particular variety, how ripe it was when it was picked, if it was kept cool or not, and how long it was on the truck or in the store. Consequently, you can't assume that every piece of organic produce is more nutritious than the conventional piece of produce sitting next to it. Theoretically it should be, but often it is not.

In addition, processing foods always diminishes the nutrient content of food and organic food is no exception. A team at the University of California Davis studied 10 tomato-based pasta sauces, half organic, half not. Although the organic tomatoes may have had more nutrients to start with, the study showed there was no real difference in nutrient content after processing.

quote: *Whereas organic foods were once truly raised naturally, on small farms with great integrity, big business has now stepped in and tainted many of the principles upon which the organic label was founded... You are in fact being ripped off by much of the organic food you are buying.*

—Dr. Joseph Mercola

is it *really* organic?

As mentioned earlier, I have a friend who often quips, "Just because it's organic doesn't mean it's good for you!" I would take that declaration a step further and say, "Just because it's labeled "organic" doesn't mean it really is organic!"

Ironically, at this moment in time there are small farmers who are compliant with all the organic practices and yet not able to label their products organic because they can't afford the federal certification process. At the same time there are major agribusiness conglomerates such as Aurora Organic and Horizon Organic dairy producers that have been violating organic standards yet boasting organic labels for years. In addition, QAI, North America's largest *for-profit* organic certifier is surrounded by controversy and accusations from critics that it's allowing companies such as these to bend, if not break, the rules.

The USDA National Organic Program which is still relatively new, is understaffed and underfunded. Consequently there is little policing going on. In the aforementioned case, it wasn't until much haranguing by the Organic Consumers Association, a non-profit watchdog organization, that the USDA finally stepped in and took action against these non-compliant dairy producers.

This is just one example of how major food corporations interested in maximizing profits are constantly trying to water down or skirt around the established definition of organic. Another example is the USDA's recent attempt to sneak 38 banned conventional ingredients into organic beer, sausage and processed foods, primarily food colorings that are supposedly not "commercially available" in organic form.

And then there are foreign imports whose organic status is frequently questionable. For example, although the USDA has yet to finalize an organic standard for farmed fish, they're allowing imported seafood, such as farmed salmon and cod, to be sold in the U.S. with an "organic" label. Similarly, an increasing number of products labeled organic are also coming into the U.S. from China even though a USDA economist admits that China is probably too polluted "to grow truly organic food."

is it pesticide- and additive-free?
In addition, just as you can't automatically assume that any given organic food product is more nutritious, you also can't automatically assume it is free of pesticide and herbicide residue or even toxic food additives.

Although organic farming by its very definition assumes that chemical fertilizers, pesticides and herbicides are not being used to produce the crop, organic crops are inadvertently exposed to pesticides, herbicides and chemical fertilizers that are now pervasive in rain and ground water and sometimes down winds due to their overuse in the past fifty years. To what degree, will once again vary from farm to farm and field to field and even crop to crop. This is something organic farmers have little to no control over.

As for health-robbing food additives, there is a relatively-new-to-the-market popular natural brand canned soup sold at all major health food stores that is labeled organic. A quick check of the ingredients list, however, reveals that it contains autolyzed yeast extract, which we learned earlier is another name for MSG. They're not the first, the last or the only supposedly natural brand food company to include this and other ingredients that cannot be considered organic by any reasonable definition, and is yet another clear demonstration of the nebulousness that now surrounds the use of term organic.

The closer a food is to its whole, fresh, natural state, the higher its nutritional value.

quote: *Making an informed produce decision at the grocery store, it turns out, is nearly impossible these days. There's no way to know where the food came from, what soils it was grown in...and which chemicals were used on it.*

—Mike Adams, *NewsTarget Insider*

what's a consumer to do?

Clearly there is no fool-proof system for assuring that you can automatically equate a product labeled organic with superior quality. As demand, profits and big industry involvement have increased, the term "organic" has increasingly become an almost meaningless buzz word that may in the past have held great value, but unfortunately today has become questionable.

So don't go bankrupt or knock yourself out in pursuit of food products sporting "organic" labels. As we have seen they may or may not be better for you or may or may not even be organic for that matter. Instead, use good judgment with each individual decision and follow the *Eating-for-Health Guidelines* when deciding what to put on your plate. Remember, as the debate rages on about whether or not organic is better, there is one point on which most everyone agrees and that is that whole, fresh and natural foods whether organic or not, are always a better choice than processed.

helpful tips & tidbits

- *Plant a garden and grow your own food!*

- *Shop at local farmer's markets and food co-ops whenever possible — the latest buzz is that "local" has become the new "organic."*

- *Make friends with the produce manager at your local health food store. Ask them when fresh produce comes in, which items are from where, and how to choose the best piece.*

- *Support all truly organic farmers and associated organizations with their endeavors to produce healthier food and a cleaner environment.*

- *Go with natural food brands that have established reputations, such as Amy's and Bob's Red Mill, whenever possible.*

- *Shy away from companies that appear to be cashing in on the booming natural foods market. Do some research, to know for sure what you're getting.*

- *Consume the <u>best quality</u> food you can afford, the highest percentage of it being whole, fresh and natural, whether it's organic or not.*

resources

- *Organic Consumers Association:* www.OrganicConsumers.org
- *Environmental Working Group:* www.ewg.org
- *United States Department of Agriculture:* www.usda.gov
- *Food Co-op Directory Service:* www.CoopDirectory.org
- *The U.S. Slow Food Movement:* www.SlowFoodUSA.org

section four

Eating-for-Health Guideline #4:
Account for Food Allergies & Sensitivities

Eating-for-Health Guideline #4:
Account for Food Allergies & Sensitivities

---

factoid: *When you conquer your food reactions, your appearance, your health, and your zest for life will improve immeasurably.*

—Elson Haas, M.D., Author

"One man's food is another man's poison" best describes the topic of food allergies. The problem of food allergies and sensitivities is quickly gaining in recognition and understanding as it has become widespread, and is associated with a multitude of symptoms and adverse health conditions. So when it comes to what's put on the table at your house, keep this all-important guideline in mind.

Simply stated *Eating-for-Health Guideline #4* is:

account for food allergies & sensitivities
…when making wise food choices.

Some experts estimate that 1 out of 3 people suffer from one or more food allergies, the majority of which go undiagnosed. I believe this is a conservative estimate as it only accounts for full-blown food allergies. Many people are eating foods, especially wheat, dairy, soy and sugar, that are causing them digestive problems, constipation, inflammation, congestion and sinus problems, depression, and otherwise upsetting the body-mind system as a result. Although these people may not show a full-blown allergy to these foods, they are nonetheless sensitive or intolerant to them on other levels.

For example, a woman once came to an *Eating-for-Health* class with multiple symptoms, the most prevalent being a persistent cough. For three years she had sought help for this condition from numerous healthcare practitioners who gave her drugs and nutritional supplements. None of these solved the problem and she had grown weary having spent much time and money trying to get relief. When she told me this, the first thing I asked was if she drank orange juice, a notoriously mucous producing food to those with allergies. (Normally I would have first asked if she consumed dairy products, but I wrongly assumed this had already been checked.) She said no, she only drank milk and water. To which I replied, "There's your problem right there."

Of course, she didn't believe me at first, thinking certainly the allergist would have come up with something that simple. Finally, I told her I would give her $100 cash if she quit drinking milk and her cough didn't subside.

She came back a week later and I could tell just by looking at her that she had quit drinking milk. The bags and dark circles under her eyes—a common indication of food allergies—had diminished significantly. When the time came, she shared with us that she had, in fact, not drank milk that week, that her cough had all but gone away and that she was really pleased that she had finally gotten to the bottom of this longstanding problem. She also expressed anger that she had consulted, at great expense, more than one medical doctor, including a top allergist, several natural healthcare practitioners and none of them had been able to uncover the cause of this persistent coughing.

"Why didn't anyone tell me?" she lamented. "If only I had known." I reminded her that I had tried to tell her earlier, but she didn't believe me. She responded that she was very grateful for my persistence and that she had finally heeded my recommendations to account for food allergies and sensitivities. (Hint, hint.) When she returned the following week, she reported that she had taken her son off milk, too. As a result, the symptoms he was having in response to this common food allergen, including bedwetting and hyperactivity, had subsided.

Accounting for food allergies and sensitivities is especially important for children as they are even more sensitive. There are so many little ones who spend the first few years of their lives suffering needlessly from a host of symptoms and *dis*-eases, including recurrent ear infections, colds and flu, skin rashes, behavior problems, digestive disturbances, and much more, which could be easily remedied by eliminating offending foods, especially wheat, soy, dairy and sugar.

Knowing this story and countless others, I can't help but wonder how many other people suffer needlessly on a daily basis or have had similar crisis situations that could have been avoided by a simple change in diet. By checking out food allergies and sensitivities as a possibility, you have nothing to lose and you may have *literally* everything to gain. It is definitely worth exploring.

Please educate yourself and get help if you need it. Be sure that you and your family are ingesting the most appropriate foods for your precious bodies and avoiding those foods to which you are intolerant. Proper nutrition is the first line of defense in preventing *dis*-ease, as well as the first line of offense in reversing it. Be aware however, that identifying and eliminating food sensitivities can be tricky business and a medical doctor is often *not* the place to go for help.

food allergy symptoms

Common symptoms associated with food allergies and sensitivities include, but are not limited to:

acne	celiac disease	irritable bowel syndrome
anxiety	colitis & diarrhea	learning disorders
arthritis	depression	mental fogginess
asthma	dermatitis	mood swings
attention deficit	diabetes	multiple sclerosis
autism	ear infections	PMS
bedwetting	gallbladder problems	schizophrenia
bronchitis	hay fever	sinusitis
candida (yeast)	headaches/migraines	skin disorders
chronic fatigue	hormonal imbalance	sleep disorders
Chron's disease	hyperactivity	tonsillitis

tricky business

When most people think of allergies, they think of breaking out in hives, a rash or having some other immediate or dramatic reaction. That is sometimes the case with food allergies, but more often it is not. The nuances of food allergies are not completely understood, but we do know that there are essentially two different kinds of reactions.

One is said to be a classic allergic response in which the body exhibits an immediate antibody reaction. The other is often referred to as a food sensitivity, in which the immune system is also triggered but in a slower, less dramatic way. As mentioned earlier, it can also happen that a person does not have an immune response to a food at all, but that particular food is nevertheless wreaking havoc on their body.

Scientific distinctions aside, to make things easy to remember for our purposes, as has become common practice, the terms food allergy, sensitivity, intolerance or reaction will be used interchangeably and will refer to any one of these three scenarios. Let the doctors and scientists quibble about specific distinctions. The bottom line for our discussion here is that no matter what you choose to call it, we are talking about foods that *don't* agree with *your* body.

People's responses and the time it takes to respond to food allergies can vary widely. Some people will develop sinus problems in reaction to an offending food, while someone else will experience a headache or stiff joints in response to the same food. Similarly, a reaction to a food may not show up in the body until a couple of days after consuming the offending food. This can throw a person off track; not ever thinking that the symptoms they are experiencing could be related to something they ate a couple of days before. This is especially true of some additives such as monosodium glutamate (MSG) which is known to cause severe symptoms, including migraine headaches, fatigue, and irritability, often not until 1-2 days after consumption.

Another problem is that people often eat the foods they are sensitive to on a daily basis and their symptoms become chronic. This is one reason people develop sensitivities to certain foods in the first place: they are *over* eaten in our culture and people develop intolerances to them as a result.

Run down this list of common food allergens and you have a profile of the typical American diet. Most Americans eat an abundance of difficult to digest, poor-quality dairy products and the same overly-processed foods (pasta, breads, cereals, pastries, baked goods, etc. — primarily made from refined gluten grains) with very little nutritional value, every day, frequently three or more times a day. Their digestive and immune systems degenerate as a result and sensitivities to these and other foods develop. It's the body's way of trying to tell you "I am *sick* of this food" — literally!

most common food allergens
The most common food allergens include, but are not limited to:

alcohol	nightshades *(eggplant, potatoes, tomatoes, etc.)*
artificial additives	peanuts
artificial sweeteners	preservatives
chocolate & cola	colorings
citrus *(esp. oranges)*	sugars *(esp. refined)*
coffee & caffeine	shellfish
corn & its derivatives	soy
dairy products *(milk, cheese, yogurt, etc.)*	strawberries
eggs	yeast
gluten grains *(wheat, spelt, oats, etc.)*	

note: *Allergies and sensitivities to beef and dairy products sometimes result from the antibiotics and hormones fed to the cows and the pasteurization of the dairy products. After switching to organic meat products and raw dairy prodcuts some people's sensitivities to these foods subside.*

The closer a food is to its whole, fresh, natural state, the higher its nutritional value.

it's not good for _you_

Blanket statements such as "whole wheat, milk or soy are _good_ for you" are commonly parroted and accepted statements. Unfortunately, these statements don't take into account the fact that these are some of the most common food allergens, causing problems among increasing numbers of people today. These foods are certainly _not_ good for those who are allergic or sensitive to them. And whether you currently show signs of being sensitive to them or not, it is not wise for anyone to consume these common food allergens daily as doing so can cause intolerances to develop.

Another issue that we are only just beginning to see the results of, is the introduction of genetically modified organisms (GMO's) into our food supply starting in the mid-90's. These largely unregulated substances are notorious for causing food allergies and estimated to be in 60-70% of foods in the U.S. today. Interestingly, in the last 10 years parallel to the introduction of GMO's, the incidence of food allergies has doubled in this country. Unfortunately, these fake foods aren't required to be listed on labels. For this reason, buy products that say "non-GMO" whenever possible.

constant craving

The body tends to _crave_ foods to which it is sensitive. The body becomes dependent on the offending food, much the same way as a smoker craves nicotine when trying to quit. Food cravings can be a form of withdrawal symptom and as such, are great indicators of food sensitivities. What foods do you crave? What foods cause you to become irritable or anxious when you go for any length of time without them? These are foods to which you are probably allergic and addicted.

It is also important to understand that most people have _multiple_ food allergies, not just one. All too often today, people who discover they are allergic to dairy, for example, substitute soy products instead. Because soy is one of the most notorious food allergens, by doing so a person is substituting one common food allergen for another; and frequently exchanging one set of symptoms for another as well. Sometimes these symptoms show up immediately and sometimes they don't develop until later. They usually show up one way or the other however, because people who are prone to food sensitivities have a weakened digestive and immune system and can't tolerate highly allergenic foods. Unfortunately, because many people think they are doing themselves a favor by switching to soy, when new symptoms show up or the old ones don't go away, they never make the connection.

I cannot stress enough the importance of discovering whether or not you are suffering from food allergies and sensitivities. A woman once commented that no one in her family had any _known_ food allergies. This same woman had earlier listed a whole litany of symptoms that she and her family had—digestive problems, headaches, joint pain, fatigue, sinus problems, and more. As I told her, if you are discounting this information thinking it doesn't apply to you, and yet you are experiencing _any_ adverse health conditions, do yourself a big favor and think again!

Whether you have known or suspected food allergies or sensitivities—or think you don't have any—follow the step-by-step instructions for a _Basic Elimination Diet_ to help you identify which foods are working for you and those you may be surprised to find are causing you problems. A _Basic Elimination Diet_ is also a great way to break the cycle of addiction to extreme, addictive foods such as refined sugars and caffeine, as well as a mild form of cleansing and rejuvenating your system that can aid healing on all levels.

Wheat:
A Problem Food for *Every*Body

As one of the most common food allergens, wheat has long been associated with a host of symptoms. Regardless of whether or not you have a known or suspected allergy, sensitivity, or intolerance to wheat, it is wise for *everyone* to limit or avoid this staple grain altogether for several reasons:

1 ~ We eat *way* too much wheat in this country. For many it's the only grain they ever eat. This is problematic because it means missing out on the many nutrients that other grains have to offer. In addition, eating the same foods over and over can tax the system, deplete specific enzymes, and lead to intolerances down the road.

2 ~ Unless you are the rare person who cooks up bowls of wheat berries, which is its whole grain form, all of the wheat being served up in this country is processed—the overwhelming majority of which, is *highly* processed into white refined flour.

White refined flour and the many products made from it – pasta, breads, cereals, pastries, cookies and more—are devoid of most vital nutrients and fiber. These foods are so devitalized they're actually *anti*-nutrients that deplete the body of vitamins, minerals, and enzymes in order to process them.

Unfortunately, even many of the products labeled "whole wheat" are themselves highly processed, and also frequently contain white refined flour and refined sugars as well. Check the label!

3 ~ Wheat in any form, processed or not, is challenging to digest and eliminate due to its high gluten content. Remember as a child mixing flour and water to make glue? It is gluten that gave this mixture its sticky, glue-like consistency.

Gluten is a mixture of gum like, water-insoluble plant proteins found in many grains, and wheat has the highest gluten content of them all. Great stuff for binding paper maché, not so good for the intestines or any other part of the digestive and eliminative tract, for that matter.

4 ~ Because it is so difficult to digest and eliminate, wheat is a notorious mucous-producer and inflammatory agent known to cause or contribute to a host of *dis*-eases, including: arthritis, sinus problems, constipation, diarrhea, bowel disorders, fatigue, yeast infections, liver and gallbladder congestion, mental disorders, insomnia, and suppressed immune function. In Chinese medicine wheat is considered one of the primary causes of depression.

There isn't any condition in the body that can't be improved by improving your diet!

Regardless of whether or not you're suffering from these or any other symptoms, everyone can benefit from limiting wheat in their diet or going completely wheat-free. Try it and see!

Today it is easier than ever before to go wheat-free or at least cut down on your intake. There is an array of wheat-free and gluten-free products now available on the market. Choose from:

gluten grains		non-gluten grains	
barley	spelt	amaranth	quinoa
kamut®	teff	buckwheat	rice
oats	wheat	corn	sorghum
rye		millet	

When you enjoy these whole grain alternatives, you will not only be giving your system a break from wheat and white refined flour, but you will also be giving your body more of the beneficial nutrients and fiber it so desperately needs. Losing some of the wheat can mean regaining some of your health and energy!

two favorite wheat-free products

My first favorite wheat-free product is spelt pasta by a company called *Vita Spelt*. They make rotini, elbows, spaghetti and even lasagne noodles in both light and dark (whole grain) varieties. This is truly my favorite pasta. It has a kind of nutty flavor. I like to mix the dark and light together. It gives the dish a little color and texture and lightens the heaviness of the whole-grain variety.

Spelt is actually a species of wheat. But because it contains less gluten and is not as hybridized as wheat itself, it is less allergenic and easier for many people to digest.

The next wheat-free delight, is *Wasa Rye Crispbread*. Spread with a bit of almond butter or unrefined virgin coconut oil for a delicious, fiber-rich snack. They make a few different kinds, some of which contain wheat. Check the label to be sure you are getting only rye. Give these products a try and see how satisfying going wheat free can be!

favorite gluten-free products
Going gluten free has gotten easier than ever too. Here's just a few favorite gluten-free items:

- *Gluten-Free Pancake Mix*, by Bob's Red Mill ~
  Tip: make extra and reheat in toaster oven for a delicious snack.

- *Brown Rice Tortillas*, by Food for Life ~
  Tip: must be heated in pan and eaten immediately or gets hard and chewy.

- *Brown Rice Pasta*, by Tinkyáda ~ *Tip:* be sure not to overcook or gets mushy.

- *Rice Sembei* (like baked chips), by Masuya ~ *Tip:* the tamari flavor is the best.

Got Milk or Dairy Products?
Why You May Want to Eliminate or Limit Them

factoid: *There are several good reasons for all of us to minimize the use of milk products whether we can "stomach" them or not...Cute milk-mustache ads aside, worldwide research increasingly indicates that milk consumption, especially in childhood, can lead to very serious problems: diabetes, heart disease, infant anemia, Crohn's disease, M.S., infertility, and asthma.*

—Julia Ross, *The Diet Cure*

Like wheat, commercial dairy products* rank as one of the most common food allergens that are also eaten *way, way* too much to be healthy in this country. There is a reason that wheat, dairy, and soy (which we will discuss next) top the list of the most common food allergens. They are difficult for the body—*any* body—to process. Once again, whether or not you have a known or suspected allergy, sensitivity, or intolerance to dairy it is wise for *everyone* to limit its consumption for several reasons.

Also similar to wheat, dairy foods are very mucous producing, which clogs the tissues and organs of the body resulting in congested and inflammatory conditions. Dairy products are most notorious for causing or exacerbating any kind of sinus or respiratory conditions, including sinusitis and asthma, and are best completely avoided whenever someone is suffering from acute respiratory ailments including bronchitis, a cold or the flu.

They are also notorious for causing acute and chronic gastrointestinal distress such as gas, bloating, constipation, diarrhea, acid reflux, and liver/gallbladder disorders. Regular or excessive consumption of dairy products can also cause weight gain, weaken the immune system, and cause or contribute to inflammatory conditions such as arthritis and bursitis.

It is important to remember that symptomatic reactions to common food allergens can manifest differently for different people and dairy is no exception. In addition to the preceding list, dairy consumption may be responsible for or contribute to *any* symptom or *dis*-ease you may be experiencing

Compounding the challenge of its allergenic nature, most commercial dairy products on the market today contain synthetic hormones and antibiotics now commonly used as part of dairy and livestock production. Ingestion of these harmful substances carry with them another whole set of problems discussed in a previous article. Because of the problems associated with hormone and antibiotic ingestion, on those occasions when you do indulge in dairy, be sure the products are organic. The few extra cents you'll pay are well worth it.

Also take into consideration that many people, depending on the nature of their sensitivity, do better with some forms of dairy than others. For example, people who are lactose intolerant often can't tolerate the more liquid forms of dairy such

No-Nonsense Nutrition

If It's Not Food, Don't Eat It!

Article Series ~ By Kelly Hayford, CNC, Author

as milk or sour cream, which have a higher lactose content, without immediate and pronounced gastric distress, but have little to no immediate trouble with hard cheeses. Experiment to see what works best for you, all the while keeping in mind that overall limitation of all forms of dairy is your healthiest choice.

I realize that this recommendation may completely contradict what you have been told since you were a small child. "Drink your milk, it's good for you" is indelibly etched upon most of our American minds. For several decades now the dairy industry has done a very good job of leading us to believe that milk and other dairy products are a staple food that we can't live without. Through relentless advertising and marketing campaigns disguised as educational in nature, they have been successful in creating a cultural climate that upholds commercial milk and dairy products as nourishing wonder foods that if excluded from the diet will result in physical calamity. However, this simply is not true.

Consult with the top experts on nutrition who base their knowledge on sound information and research, rather than parroting marketing ploys, and you will find few who disagree with the notion of limiting the amount of dairy, including milk, in one's diet. For example, Dr. Walter Willett, a trained physician and current head of Harvard's Department of Nutrition, states in his recent book, *Eat, Drink, and Be Healthy*, "...there are more reasons *not* to drink milk in large amounts than there are to drink it. I don't recommend it as a beverage for adults and believe you should think of milk as an optional food..."

factoid: *In the U.S., the average per capita consumption of dairy products is 580 lbs. per person a year.*

osteoporosis, calcium & dairy products

With regard to the issue of adequate calcium intake, once again I refer to Dr. Walter Willett's book, *Eat, Drink, and Be Healthy*, which contains an entire chapter on this topic entitled *Calcium: No Emergency*. This informative chapter debunks the myth that we are a country suffering from an acute lack of calcium resulting in high rates of osteoporosis. Dr. Willett points to the *National Dairy Council* advertising campaigns as the source of this myth, which has been expounded upon by the supplement industry pushing the latest and greatest source of calcium in convenient pill form.

"For starters, there isn't a calcium emergency. When it comes to calcium in the diet, the United States is near the top of the list of per capita calcium intake, second only to some Scandinavian Countries and parts of Latin America...," Dr. Willett states in this chapter. "Unfortunately, there's little proof that just boosting your calcium intake to the high levels that are currently recommended will prevent fractures. And all the high-profile attention given to calcium is distracting us from strategies that really work....Curiously, countries with the highest average calcium intake tend to have higher, not lower, hip fracture rates," he goes on to say.

We don't have to look far to see proof of this. Many cultures eat little to no dairy foods and yet have very low rates of osteoporosis. Asian cultures are a good example.

If you are not convinced and are still concerned about getting enough calcium, there are many other foods that provide even *more* calcium than dairy products, and in a much more bioavailable form. Green foods and sea vegetables are two such foods. They can be included in your meals and also taken as whole food supplements. More importantly, educate yourself about the *real* causes of osteoporosis and safe natural ways to prevent and reverse it.

The biggest contributor to osteoporosis is our poor-quality, modern diets that create an acidic condition in the body that then leaches calcium from the bones to neutralize the acidity. The over consumption of refined sugars and soda are two of the biggest culprits in this process. Refined sugars in general because they are very acidifying, and soda especially because it not only contains high-fructose corn syrup, one of the worst refined sugars, but also phosphoric acid which further acidifies the system. The over consumption of commercial dairy products themselves can contribute to the development of osteoporosis because they increase acidity in the body as well.

In addition, we are not getting the nutrients our bodies need. We are overfed but malnourished in this country and increasingly around the industrialized world. Malnourished bodies are weakened and more prone to *dis*-ease of every kind. Fresh fruits and vegetables are what's most missing in our diets. In fact, a recent study from the *Elsie Widdowson Laboratory, MRC Human Nutrition Research*, in Cambridge, UK shows that eating more fruits and vegetables increases bone density in both children and adults.

Another topic of importance is estrogen dominance and progesterone deficiency. Estrogen is involved with the process of breaking down old bone, while progesterone is involved in the process of building new bone. Some experts say most women (and men) today suffer from lack of progesterone caused by poor diet and environmental factors. For more on this important topic, please go to: www.JohnLeeMD.com

factoid: *...dairy products shouldn't occupy the prominent place that they do in the USDA Food Pyramid, nor should they be the centerpiece of the national strategy to prevent osteoporosis.*

—Dr. Walter Willett
Chairman, *Dept. of Nutrition Harvard School of Public Health*

alternatives to dairy

As far as what to put on your cereal in the morning, one of the best alternatives is oat milk. Among the dairy alternatives, to many people it has a taste and texture that is most like cow's milk. Some people can't even tell the difference. Almond or rice are two other recommended choices. I do not recommend soy milk, however, as it is another common food allergen.

Keep in mind that most of these milk substitutes are highly processed and not always the best or most nourishing choice for the body. When you do buy these milk substitutes, be sure to check the label and always buy the brand with the best overall ingredients and the least amount of added sweeteners. The original or plain variety is usually your best bet where sugar content is concerned. Cold, dry, sugary sweet cereal with cow's milk or even milk substitute is one of the worst choices for starting the day anyway. Use these alternatives as transition foods or once-in-awhile treats, and gradually move onto even healthier choices. Water, tea, and *fresh* fruit and vegetable juices are your best choice for beverages.

Goat's milk and goat cheese is another alternative for some people. It is generally easier to digest and less taxing to the body than cow's milk, but still wise to keep to a minimum. Coconut milk is another fabulous alternative that is at the top of my list along with coconut oil. In Thailand people

The closer a food is to its whole, fresh, natural state, the higher its nutritional value.

drink coconut milk with the same frequency that we drink cow's milk in this country, and have comparatively low rates of obesity, heart disease, and osteoporosis. They're obviously doing something right and we could take some pointers.

As for other cheese substitutes, I haven't found any good choices. There are a variety of substitutes now on the market usually made from either soy, almonds, rice, or oats. But quite frankly, none of them comes anywhere near the taste or texture of the real stuff and I'm not convinced that they are any better for you than the cheese you're trying to avoid. Try cheese alternatives and see if they do anything for you, being mindful that they are processed foods and best kept to a minimum.

Or consider doing what I do, which is to do without the substitutes and enjoy a bit of raw, organic cheese 1-3 times a week in keeping with this notion of having dairy on a limited basis. For some people it may be wise to have it even less or not at all. Experiment to find what's best for you, and know that whatever you discover may change in the future as your body changes. Whatever you do, keep your commercial dairy consumption well below the culturally-popular 580 pounds per capita consumption if you want to restore or maintain your health, energy, and natural weight!

factoid : *Contrary to advertising, dairy products are not even a desirable source of calcium…*
In cattle tests, calves given their own mother's milk that had first been pasteurized, didn't live six weeks!

— Linda Page, N.D., *Healthy Healing*

*commercial dairy products versus raw, unpasteurized

It's important to make a clear distinction between *commercial* dairy products—which is what the overwhelming majority of people are consuming in America today—and traditional dairy products that are not pasteurized and come from pasture-fed cows free of hormones and antibiotics.

The pasteurization process uses heat that alters the nature of the milk protein and renders it harmful to the body. Commercial dairy farms also use massive amounts of toxic hormones and antibiotics (See *Section 1* for more on hormones and antibiotics.) Before the vast commercialization of dairy products and its unhealthy practices, the rate of allergies to dairy products was very low. Many people who are allergic to commercial dairy products have little or no problem with traditional raw dairy products. Give them a try.

Raw milk and dairy products are available in retail stores and farmer's markets in some states. In others, you can get them straight from the farm by buying a share in a cow. This is also a great way to get organic, grass-fed meats.

For farms that offer this service in your area and more information on the problems associated with commercial dairy products and the benefits of raw dairy products from pasture-fed cows, visit:

- www.NotMilk.com
- www.WestonAPrice.com
- www.RealMilk.com

No-Nonsense Nutrition

Article Series ~ By Kelly Hayford, CNC, Author *If It's Not Food, Don't Eat It!*

Soy — Oh, Boy!

Things to Consider About This Not-Always-Healthy Health Food

food factoid: *60% of processed foods contain soy or soy derivatives.*

People frequently ask me about soy expecting that I will respond with a simple "it's good" or "it's bad" for you. It's like asking if potatoes are good for you and if I say yes, surmising from there that potatoes in any form from French fries to potato chips to Pringles are, therefore, good for you.

Since of course this is not the case, instead I reply with a sigh, and then say "soy — oh, boy!" — because the answer is a little more complicated than it's "good" or "bad" for you. To simplify and separate fact from fiction, following are some things to consider about soy.

things to consider about soy:

1 ~ Soy is one of the top five most common food allergens because it contains a protein enzyme inhibitor that prevents it and other nutrients from being properly digested. People with compromised digestive, eliminative, and immune function are especially susceptible. Symptoms range from digestive disturbances such as gas and bloating to severe depression and anxiety — and every other conceivable symptom that may be associated with food allergies or sensitivities. Regardless of any health benefits you may have heard associated with soy, if you have an allergy or intolerance to soy and can't digest it properly (and many Westerners can't!) it won't do you any good and may in fact be causing you harm.

2 ~ Fifty-four percent of America's soybean crop is genetically engineered (GE or GMO) and contains 27% more trypsin inhibitor, meaning that it has even greater potential for setting off allergic reactions and digestive disturbances. In 1998 the UK reported a 50% increase in food allergies and attributed this dramatic rise to the fact that consumers the previous year had started eating large amounts of imported GE soybeans. (See *Section 1* for more on the problems with genetically engineered crops or GMO's.)

3 ~ Soy is best consumed in a fermented form such as miso, tempeh, natto and soy or tamari sauce. Fermentation reduces soybean's enzyme inhibitors to some degree, and is therefore much easier to digest and less likely to cause reactions. There are also fermented soy protein powders now available at health food stores. Sprouted soy and edamame (green soybean) are also easier to digest and assimilate and a much better choice. Tofu, which is known to block mineral abosorption, is best eaten warm with a little fish or other animal protein to offset this effect and increase digestibility.

4 ~ Products such as soy flour, soy powders other than the fermented or sprouted variety, soy grits, soy flakes, soy nuts, and soy nut butter are best avoided as they

Section 4, No. 4

Copyright 2008
Kelly Hayford

There isn't any condition in the body that can't be improved by improving your diet!

Fresh edamame (green soybean).

have not had the trypsin inhibitor removed and are therefore highly allergenic. Super-refined soy products, such as soybean oil, textured soy protein (TSP), and textured vegetable protein (TVP) are also not recommended as the soy is subjected to high pressure, high temperatures and/or caustic chemicals as part of the processing. Soy cheeses and soy milks are often highly refined and best avoided as well. Milks made from oats, rice, almonds and coconut are a better choice.

5 ~ Asian women have very low rates of menopausal complaints, heart disease, breast cancer and osteoporosis. The soy industry, with sketchy evidence to support their claims, attributes this to soy being a regular part of the Asian diet. These claims, that have become widely accepted due to massive media campaigns, disregard extensive research that shows otherwise. They also disregard other dietary and lifestyle factors at play in Asian cultures.

For example, there are many Asian populations that don't eat soy as a regular part of their diet, yet still enjoy low rates of the *dis*-eases mentioned. Among those who do eat soy regularly, fermented soy products are what is consumed the most. Asians aren't downing quarts of overly-sweetened, highly-processed soy milk or popping supplements containing concentrated soy isoflavones, as is becoming popular in this country.

In addition, the traditional Asian diet consists of primarily whole, fresh, natural foods including sea vegetables, which are packed with vital nutrients and one of the richest sources of absorbable calcium. They also eat a lot of fish, small amounts of meat, and little to no dairy products or processed foods in stark contrast to the *Standard American Diet*, which consists of mostly processed foods high in sugar, fat, sodium, and excessive amounts of meat and *zero* sea vegetables.

6 ~ Soy reduces thyroid hormone slowing metabolism and is therefore not appropriate for those who are hypothyroid or wanting to lose weight. Sea vegetables on the other hand stimulate the thyroid and are frequently combined with soy in Asian cuisine such as miso soup, which results in the two counterbalancing one another.

7 ~ As with any of the most common food allergens (wheat, dairy, soy, corn, etc.), if you choose to include soy in your diet, do so on a rotational basis eating it about once every 4-5 days (never daily!) in the user-friendly forms described above. This will allow the body adequate processing time and reduce the likelihood of developing or exacerbating sensitivities and other problems.

Much of the hoopla about the benefits of soy isn't based on good science, but rather the interests of a booming industry that's making a gold mine on a cheap, versatile, highly-profitable commodity. Don't fall prey to these antics. As with any common food allergens, if you include soy in your diet be sure it agrees with *your* body and you're eating the most bioavailable and non-GMO forms.

resources
For more information on this topic, read: *The Whole Soy Story*, by Kaayla T. Daniel.

No-Nonsense Nutrition

Article Series ~ By Kelly Hayford, CNC, Author *If It's Not Food, Don't Eat It!*

Basic Elimination Diet ~ Part 1
Clear Cravings/Addictions & Identify Food Sensitivities

Many healthcare practitioners advocate following an elimination diet in order to give the digestive system a rest, help clear the bowels, identify food allergies and sensitivities, and breaking the cycle of addiction to certain foods and stimulants.

In a nutshell, an elimination diet involves eliminating all common food allergens and any other foods that you suspect may be a problem for you. When used as a tool for testing for food intolerances, after an initial 5-7 days on a strict elimination diet, you then reintroduce one suspect food at a time over the course of the following few days or weeks, taking careful note of any reactions to these foods as you add them back into your diet (see *Food Allergy Testing*).

An elimination diet can be followed for any number of days depending on the results you're trying to achieve. Many people go on an elimination diet for a day or two to help restore balance after holiday partying, for example. Or do it for a week as a part of a regular internal Spring-cleaning. If you're trying to clear cravings, identify food intolerances, or otherwise reverse any kind of chronic condition however, following an elimination diet for a minimum of 21 days is best.

When done correctly, adhering to a basic elimination diet for 21 days or more is a life-changing experience that will alter your relationship with food. Many people who thought they had no sensitivities to foods are amazed to discover that certain foods are indeed causing them symptoms and *dis*-eases of one kind or another. As their system starts to clear out accumulated sludge, they're also amazed at how much better they feel. In addition to the reduction or elimination of food cravings and nagging symptoms, increased energy and clarity of mind are what people most often report after being on an elimination diet. Give yourself this opportunity to discover just how good you can feel!

basic elimination diet step-by-step

1 ~ *strategize* the process before you begin
… to set yourself up for success in every area.

Prepare yourself in every way to ensure your success. As mentioned earlier, 21 days is the best, especially if you want to test for food intolerances. It is wise to practice and work up to this, however. Start with one or two days (preferably on the weekend) to get a feel for what will be required in terms of food preparation and how your body will respond.

When you're ready, check your calendar and schedule the full 21-day elimination diet when there will be little to no outside distractions such as travel or significant social engagements. Clean sweep your kitchen of any foods you may crave in the initial stages. It wouldn't be an effective treatment plan to try and rehabilitate an addict with a refrigerator and cupboards filled with their drug of choice.

During the program, think at least a day ahead and always have food ready to take with you if needed. Don't be caught somewhere without any healthy food choices and be forced to go hungry or resort to something you don't want to eat. Follow the elimination diet exactly as described 100% of the time for maximum benefits and to get as accurate a reading as possible when testing for food sensitivities. Also, be aware that this is a *general* elimination diet. It can be modified further to address specific conditions such as candida, arthritis, gluten intolerance, or blood sugar problems.

2 ~ do not eat any common food allergens
...or foods to which you suspect you may be sensitive or may have trouble digesting or eliminating.

This is what an elimination diet is all about: going off all common food allergens, which are generally notorious for causing problems, and any other foods that you suspect may specifically be causing you trouble. This would include, but not be limited to:

- wheat
- soy
- yeast
- vinegar
- chocolate
- coffee
- corn
- eggs

- peanuts
- oranges
- strawberries
- tomatoes
- potatoes
- shellfish
- sugar/concentrated sweeteners
- all dairy products (*milk, cheese, yogurt, butter, sour cream, etc.*)

Refer back to the *Suggested Foods* lists in *Section 3* and you will see all of these common food allergens marked by parentheses. You will find other foods in parentheses and may consider eliminating them as well such as berries and cashews, which are sometimes known to cause allergic reactions, or avocados and bananas, which are difficult for some people to digest. If you suspect that you have a problem with gluten, in addition to wheat you may also want to cut out all gluten grains. If you have blood sugar problems or candida, substitute the fruit with 2-3 more servings of non-starchy vegetables. In addition to the above-mentioned common food allergens, make a clear list of all foods you suspect may be problematic and intend to eliminate and test for.

3 ~ eat at least the following every day
...excluding the above-mentioned common food allergens and those on your list of suspects:

- 6-8 glasses pure (not tap) water
- 2-3 servings fruit (fresh, cooked or raw, not dried)
- 3 servings raw or cooked *non-starchy* vegetables
- 1 serving whole grains or starches
- 1 serving animal protein
- Or if vegetarian – 1 serving beans, lentils, nuts or seeds, or a *non-allergenic* protein powder such as rice protein (no whey or soy protein powders, until you have tested them)
- At least 1 tbsp and not more than 4 tbsp extra virgin olive oil, coconut oil or sesame oil.
- Optional: small handful of *crispy* or *raw, unsalted* nuts or seeds once or twice daily

Unless you're not that hungry, consume at least the number of servings indicated above and more if you need to. You may eat whatever size portions you desire, but eat them in about these same ratios so as not to upset the overall balance. Don't, for example, eat 4 bananas and 6 cups of rice a day, as a client of mine once did, then wonder why you get constipated!

If you are really hungry or weak, be sure to include more concentrated foods, such as protein or starches. Because the whole, fresh, natural foods you'll be eating are high-octane fuel for the body, you'll metabolize and digest them much faster than the foods you normally eat. As a result, many people will be eating more food, more frequently than usual. Be sure to eat more if you are hungry, especially non-starchy vegetables and protein if you need it.

4 ~ keep meals and snacks simple
...and avoid processed foods and foods you don't normally eat.

It is best to not eat processed foods at all during your elimination diet. If you must, be sure to check the label carefully. Eating only whole, fresh, natural foods is the most cleansing and healing to the body. Take this opportunity to experience their magic first hand. Also, do not eat a lot of things that you don't normally eat (such as collard greens, beets or beans) as you may have a cleansing reaction to that particular food, making it more challenging to narrow things down when it comes to testing. Please see the next article for specific meal planning and recipes ideas.

5 ~ test for food allergies and intolerances
...by introducing them one at a time, starting on day 6.

If you choose to follow the program to the letter, do not eat any food on the list throughout the program. If you choose to test for food allergies and intolerances, Stay off all common food allergens and other foods you want to test for the first five days. It's very important that you don't consume even a trace amount of the foods that you want to test for as this can skew your results.

On the 6th day, introduce one food back into your diet, such as wheat, for example, and take note of any reactions or changes in the way you feel. Some people will notice symptoms immediately, others may not notice anything until the next day, and some will not notice anything at all.

After testing a particular food, if you *did not* have a reaction and are *confident* that it's not a problem for you, you may now include it as part of your overall elimination diet for the remainder of your program. You may then go on to test another food the next day, and proceed testing for foods in this same manner, introducing them one at a time. If you *do* have a reaction to a food you test, continue to exclude this food for the remainder of your program. Also wait a day before you test for the next food to allow your system time to clear from the reaction. Please follow the upcoming detailed instructions for *Food Allergy Testing* for best results.

6 ~ what to expect as you proceed
...can vary from person to person and may include feeling worse before you feel better.

Many people start feeling better right away, while others may be uncomfortable for the first couple days or so. Symptoms can range from mild to severe and include *headache, fatigue, nausea, vomiting, diarrhea, constipation, skin eruptions, muscle aches and pains, loss of appetite, fever, coughing, runny nose, itchy or twitchy eyes, depression, and mood swings.* But any symptom can be associated with this detoxification process, often referred to as a "healing crisis."

Most people only experience these symptoms 2-7 days. Everyone is different and how your body responds will depend on many variables, such as age, weight, current state of health, genetics, diet and lifestyle factors. In general, those who are in poor health with the worst diets usually experience the most severe symptoms. Don't let these symptoms confuse you. A healing crisis is a normal reaction to an elimination diet or any kind of cleansing.

Filling out the *Symptoms Questionnaire* (see *Section 7*) before you begin and at regular intervals throughout, is a great way to assess your overall experience with the elimination diet and the benefits you will undoubtedly receive.

The closer a food is to its whole, fresh, natural state, the higher its nutritional value.

If you haven't already weaned yourself off stimulants such as sugars and caffeine or common food allergens such as wheat and dairy products, following this *Basic Elimination Diet* is a great way to get the job done. In this case, you may experience strong cravings during the first few days. These cravings will go away if you push through to the other side of the process. The symptoms they create however, such as fatigue, excess weight, digestive problems, etc., will last *forever* as long as you keep eating the foods that are causing them! Keep this in mind to help you through.

If you feel up to it, gentle exercise such as walking, yoga, Tai Chi, or stretching will also help you through. Now is not the time for strenuous exercise, however. In fact, at least for the first few days of an elimination diet, rest and quiet time is best.

7 ~ consider modifying the program
...for practice or to best suit your needs at this time.

Set yourself up to succeed. Before you begin, really think about the time you have available, financial considerations (buying all fresh, natural foods in big quantities may cost more than what you're used to), upcoming social events, etc. If you think that the program as outlined above may be a stretch, then think about what would be more manageable to start. Here are some examples:

- *Eliminate common food allergens for 2-3 days a week.*
- *Eliminate all stimulants, especially those you struggle with (i.e., coffee, sugar, etc.)*
- *Eliminate one or more foods you suspect cause you problems (wheat, dairy, soy, etc.)*
- *Follow the guidelines above for 1-2 meals a day.*
- *Eliminate all processed, packaged foods.*

Keep in mind however, that each time you eat an addictive food you're perpetuating an existing chemical imbalance. As a result, your body may crave it more, leading to a yo-yo effect, going back and forth but never breaking free. This can be discouraging and make you feel even worse. In which case, going for the 21-day *Basic Elimination Diet* may be the solution.

8 ~ to end your program
...be sure to review, revise and recommit to what you'll do next.

Although you may have the desire to go out and scarf down a double-cheese pizza and guzzle a few sodas or beers at the end of the 21-days—*don't!* Instead: *review how things went for you, revise what you're doing to better suit your current needs, and then recommit to what will be the next phase.* The next phase you choose is up to you. Many people are inspired by the way they feel and have no desire to go through withdrawal from bad food symptoms again, which makes them want to continue at least some of what they have been doing. Don't just let things fizzle, however. Be sure to make a clear commitment for a specified amount of time for what you'll do next until the desired changes have been integrated as lifestyle habits.

Be persistent and consistent. Remember that it takes practice before you learn to play the piano and a few tries before most people are able to quit smoking. Apply what you have learned here over and over if you need to. That's what all the people I know who have been successful at integrating a healthier eating lifestyle have done. What you can look forward to is a clearer, stronger, revitalized body and mind!

No-Nonsense Nutrition

Article Series ~ By Kelly Hayford, CNC, Author *If It's Not Food, Don't Eat It!*

Basic Elimination Diet Part 2:
What to Eat?

When first embarking on a *Basic Elimination Diet* it is often easier to think about what you *can* eat as opposed to what you *can't*. Most of you will be eating very differently from what you're used to. Overall, you want to keep your meals and snacks simple, and follow food-combining principles as much as possible to insure adequate digestion and elimination.

If you've been eating the *Standard American Diet* for the most part, your taste buds are used to *un*natural foods and your tastebuds will no doubt go through some adjustments. Let go of taste being a top priority and instead think of the foods you're eating as being medicinal to help you through the initial stages. Soon you will acclimate and develop a taste for foods in their more natural state.

If you intend to test for food sensitivities, the first five days will be the most challenging. You will be eating primarily fruits, vegetables, rice and some fresh animal protein. It will get easier as you test for foods and can then add them back into your diet. It's also very important to be sure not to eat foods that you rarely, if ever have as you may have a cleansing reaction to them that would make it difficult to decipher which food is causing a particular symptom.

All produce should be fresh and organic whenever possible. Frozen would be the next best choice and good to have on hand as back up (check the label for additives). Canned foods are processed foods and devoid of vital life force energy and it's best to avoid them altogether. However, you may want to keep a couple of low sodium, allergen- and additive-free canned soups on hand (*Shelton's Chicken & Rice* is a good one) for emergency situations when you have no time to make something fresh.

There are brands of bread, rice tortillas and crackers that are free of wheat, yeast and vinegar. These are good to keep on hand as well. Be sure to check the label for unwanted ingredients and keep these processed foods to a minimum.

Meats, poultry and fish should also be whole, fresh, natural and organic whenever possible. No processed meat products such as sausage or hot dogs. Also, check labels on fresh poultry especially to be sure there are no additives if it has been pre-packaged.

At least for the duration of the elimination diet, it's helpful if you can change your ideas of what is normal to eat for breakfast or have as a snack in order to expand the possibilities for what there is to eat. General suggestions for what to eat include the following:

breakfast: *whole grain hot cereal (rice, oats, quinoa, or millet); chicken, turkey, steak, or eggs (after you have tested for them); raw or steamed fruit; baked yam, salad or bowl of steamed veggies; small handful of raw or crispy nuts.*

Section 4, No. 6

Copyright 2008
Kelly Hayford

lunch/dinner: *whole grains (rice, quinoa, or millet); chicken, turkey, steak, or eggs (after you have tested for them); baked yam or sweet potato; fresh salad or bowl of mixed steamed veggies; lentils, mung beans or other easy to digest legume, wraps made with rice tortilla, rice pasta with steamed veggies; sushi.*

snacks: *carrot juice; piece of fruit; apple with a little almond butter; raw veggie sticks and mashed avocado; a handful of nuts; millet/rice bread or wheat-free rye cracker with a little almond butter or virgin coconut oil; cup of herbal tea.*

salad dressings: *squirt of fresh lemon juice with a drizzle of olive oil; fresh garlic and lemon juice with olive oil and tahini; mashed avocado; olive oil and balsamic vinegar (after you have tested for vinegar).*

condiments: *fresh or dried herbs; sea salt; Bragg's Sprinkle seasoning blend; Trader Joe's 21-Seasoning Salute; Bragg's Liquid Aminos (if test O.K. for soy).*

beverages: *water; caffeine-free herbal tea; carrot and other fresh vegetable juices; fresh fruit juices (never bottled) diluted by half to maintain steady blood sugar levels.*

be prepared

Being prepared is the key to success for an elimination diet. For most of you, going on an elimination diet will require much more planning, preparation and food shopping than you're used to doing. Familiarize yourself with the food shopping and preparation tips in *Section 6* for more help. For specific allergen-free recipes see the recipe section of *If It's Not Food, Don't Eat It!*, by Kelly Hayford or check out the *Guilt-Free Indulgence* cookbook, by Mark and Cheri Percival.

Most of you will also be eating more than you usually do because the non-allergenic, all-natural foods you'll be having burn through your system much quicker. So it's imperative that you be thinking ahead on a daily basis so that you have enough food on hand. Preparing food the night before or in the morning for the whole day is helpful. Plan to take food with you wherever you go.

Also be sure you have lots of glass or plastic containers for storing food and taking with you. A thermal food bag or small cooler is a good idea, especially in the hot summer months. You might also consider investing in a vacuum sealer. It's a convenient device that will save you much time

and money when on an elimination diet and beyond. In fact, I believe it's a must for every healthy kitchen.

As mentioned, if you have never done an elimination diet before it's a good idea to prepare yourself further by practicing a couple days or otherwise working up to it with a modified program to begin. And remember, anything and everything you do with respect to an elimination diet will increase your understanding and experience of healthier habits in your daily eating lifestyle—so relax and enjoy the process!

No-Nonsense Nutrition

Article Series ~ By Kelly Hayford, CNC, Author *If It's Not Food, Don't Eat It!*

Food Allergy Testing Instructions

Follow the step-by-step instructions for the *Basic Elimination Diet.* Before beginning the food allergy testing phase make a list of all the common food allergens and any foods you crave, have a problem digesting or suspect may be a problem for you in any way. Narrow the list down to the foods you eat most frequently. Put them in the order you want to test them.

It's best to put the most common food allergens that you eat the most at the bottom of the list (wheat, dairy, etc.) and wait until the end of the program to test for them. This gives the body a break and helps to truly clear any symptoms, especially chronic symptoms you may have associated with these foods.

Be sure not to eat *any* common food allergens and other foods you want to test for the first five days of the program. It's critical that you don't consume even a *trace* amount of the foods that you want to test, as this can skew your results.

On the sixth day, introduce one food back into your diet. Use the *purest* form of the food possible such as those listed on the next page. Have at least 2 tablespoons (except sugar, only have 1-2 *teaspoons*.) but not more than a moderate serving at the end of each meal. Take note of any reactions or changes in the way you feel using the *Food Sensitivity Reaction Chart.*

Some people will notice symptoms immediately, such as headache, bloating, gastrointestinal distress, fatigue, depression, irritability, etc., while others may not notice anything until the next day, such as constipation, puffiness or bags under the eyes, trouble sleeping, etc., and some won't notice anything at all.

In many cases, not noticing anything at all is an indication that the food you tested is not a problem for you, but not always. It's important to understand that while it is often the case that someone is able to ferret out a specific food that is causing certain problems, because there are so many variables, sometimes this is not the case. Sometimes people's systems are so weakened and backed up from years of poor eating habits that they have to cleanse their system to a degree before they can get a true reading of what specific foods are causing them trouble.

In this case, not noticing anything after testing a food may also indicate that you need to do additional cleansing and stay off the suspect food for a longer period of time. Then re-introduce the food in two or three weeks, for example, and see how your body reacts. Feeling better when not eating a particular food is also a testament to the possible effects it may be having. Pay more attention to your body's signals, use your intuition, and experiment to know what's best for you.

After you have tested for a particular food, if you *did not* have a reaction and are confident that it is not a problem for you, you may now include it as part of your overall elimination diet for the remainder of your program. You may then go on to test another food the next day, and proceed testing for foods in this same manner for the duration of the 21 days, introducing them one at a time.

Section 4, No. 7

Copyright 2008
Kelly Hayford

if you *do* have a reaction

If you *do* have a reaction to the food you tested, continue to exclude this food for the remainder of your program. Also, wait at least a day before you test for the next food to allow your system time to recover from the reaction. Do the following, especially if you have a severe reaction:

1 ~ Take 1 level teaspoonful of baking soda in 10 ounces of water on an empty stomach. This may be done up to 3 times in a day.

2 ~ Drink plenty of water and eat minimally — fruits, vegetables and rice. Introduce more substantial foods only when the reaction has completely subsided.

3 ~ Irrigate the colon by giving yourself an enema or having a professional colonic.

forms of food to use for testing:

wheat ~ *Cream of Wheat* hot cereal and wheat tortillas that don't contain yeast.

milk ~ whole cow's milk, plain yogurt and sour cream.

cheese ~ test cheese seperately from milk, any form you usually eat.

eggs ~ any form you usually eat without other common food allergens.

soy ~ tofu, tempeh, soy milk, wheat-free tamari, miso. Test Bragg's Aminos seperately.

oranges ~ fresh oranges, orange juice. Eat or drink separate from meals.

corn ~ tortillas, corn syrup in tea or hot cereal or small spoonful.

tomatoes ~ fresh tomatoes, tomato sauce, tomato juice with no added vinegar.

potatoes ~ baked or boiled.

coffee ~ the kind you usually drink — black, no milk, sugar, creamer, etc..

chocolate ~ get the highest percentage cacao you can find and no additives.

white refined sugar ~ have 1-2 teaspoonsful in tea or by the spoonful or packet.

yeast ~ heat Fleischmann's or Red Star baker's yeast in oven at 300° for 15 minutes.
Take ¼ teaspoonful in water at the beginning of each meal.

after the elimination diet

In general, it is best to limit all common food allergens in your diet, especially wheat, dairy and soy, only having them on a rotational basis about every 4-5 days, even if you don't react to them. You will especially want to do this for any foods you have eliminated for an extended period of time, to avoid increasing or resumption of symptoms.

Common food allergens trigger the body. If you don't eat them for an extended period of time the body can heal. Much like a wound, if you keep scraping it, it will never heal. If you leave it alone, however, it can repair itself. For this reason, some people are able to successfully clear food intolerances, or at least greatly reduce their reactions to them, by eliminating any offensive foods for 6-9 months or longer while at the same time cleansing, nourishing, and strengthening their body and immune systems with natural, nutrient-rich foods, herbs, and whole food supplements.

Food Sensitivity Reaction Chart

Day	Time	Food	Pulse Before	Pulse After	Digestion (belching/ bloating, etc.)	Bowel Function (constipation/loose stools, color, etc.)	Headache/ Brain Fog/ Mood/Sleep	Sinus/Chest Congestion/ Drainage	Kidney/ Bladder Function	Eyes (puffy, dark circles, itchy)	Energy Level scale of 1-10

Food Sensitivity Reaction Chart

Day	Time	Food	Pulse Before	Pulse After	Digestion (belching/ bloating, etc.)	Bowel Function (constipation/loose stools, color, etc.)	Headache/ Brain Fog/ Mood/Sleep	Sinus/Chest Congestion/ Drainage	Kidney/ Bladder Function	Eyes (puffy, dark circles, itchy)	Energy Level scale of 1-10

section five

Eating-for-Health Guideline #5:
Account for Ailments When Making Food Choices

No-Nonsense Nutrition

Article Series ~ By Kelly Hayford, CNC, Author *If It's Not Food, Don't Eat It!*

Eating-for-Health Guideline #5:
Account for Ailments When Making Food Choices

factoid: *Drugs may change the blood chemistry, but they can not rebuild or replace tissue. Only foods can do that.*

—Dr. Bernard Jensen

There isn't any condition in the body that can't be improved by improving your diet. There isn't any condition in the body that can't be improved by improving your diet. No, the cut and paste button on my computer didn't get stuck. This is a line I rattled off during a seminar one day, a line I think is worth repeating.

It's a line worth repeating because the simple truth of it has either been lost, forgotten, or never understood amidst the high-tech, commercially-oriented mumbo jumbo of our world today. The highly-processed fake foods laid out by giant food corporations have contributed enormously to the abysmal standards of health in this and other countries, which has in turn contributed enormously to the burgeoning pharmaceutical companies and medical industry.

Indeed, on closer examination, they would appear to be feeding off of one another. Eat our bad food, get indigestion, go to the doctor, take our over-the-counter or prescription antacid, etc. All the while ignoring the original cause. This turn of events over the past few decades has led to a warped perspective of health and how to restore and maintain it. It's a warped perspective because it's based on misinformation and disillusion with regard to the *real* causes of *dis*-eased conditions and what to do about them.

taking this for that

One example of this warped perspective has to do with the way in which we have been lulled by the medical industry into believing that we can take this or that drug to eradicate this or that condition. And the natural healthcare industry isn't much better.

Many alternative healthcare providers perpetuate the 'taking this for that' mentality by substituting natural supplements for drugs, sending people off with a bag full of them without ever addressing or adequately addressing the diet and lifestyle from which the person's problems emanate.

The fact is, with rare exception, *dis*-ease in the body is caused by poor eating and lifestyle habits that then create a compromised, degenerated internal environment. It is by reversing this damage and at the same time, discontinuing the habits that caused it in the first place, that we can bring about true healing.

In the case of infants and young children who seemingly haven't been around long enough to develop *dis*-ease, their bodies are merely a product and perpetuation of the poor condition of the parents who bred them. In either case, taking drugs or natural supplements without changing the dietary and lifestyle habits

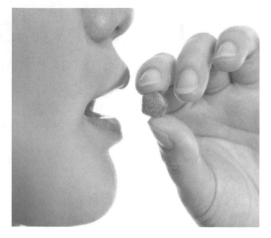

that are *causing* the condition is like rearranging the furniture on the Titanic or putting water in a bucket that has a hole in it.

Certainly there are many natural supplements that can contribute to the restoration of health and wellness, but these remedies are the icing on the cake, not the cake itself. The cake itself is what you're putting into and doing, or not doing with your body and mind on a regular basis. All *truly* holistic healing approaches to health include altering the diet and lifestyle habits that contributed to, or caused the health problems in the first place.

Food is the most effective, and yet most neglected healing tool. Food recreates your biological condition on a daily basis, either building it up or breaking it down. Many people go doctor and healer hopping, spending oodles of time and money searching everywhere for the magic panacea that will cure what ails them (I know I did!), never realizing that the cure doesn't reside in a bottle or procedure, but rather in their kitchen and unhealthful living habits.

If you're in search of assistance in relieving or eliminating symptoms or *dis*-eases, you can save yourself a tremendous amount of time, money, energy and frustration by following this and all the other *Eating-for-Health Guidelines*.

food is powerful!

My personal experience is that out of all the drugs, tests, medical procedures, herbs, supplements, healing modalities, etc., to which I was subjected, the single most powerful influence in my recovery from chronic illness was FOOD! As I have continued to eat predominately for health and refine my individual dietary needs, I keep getting stronger, healthier, clearer, and have more and more energy. Scores of other people have had similar experiences.

Doctors, drugs, herbs, vitamins, or other supplements do not heal the body. The body heals itself. The foods you eat either help or hinder this healing process. A longstanding poor diet over a number of years, which has become the norm in our modern Western world, is the root cause of the overwhelming majority of symptoms and *dis*-eases people experience.

Therefore, if you are experiencing *any* health conditions or afflictions, no matter what they are, the best thing you can do to help your body heal itself and restore a balanced state of well being is to implement this fifth *Eating-for-Health Guideline ~ account for ailments when making wise food choices*.

By doing so you're giving your body every advantage possible in its quest to heal, at least in the nutrition arena. Reducing stress, exercising, making amends with the past, enjoying loving relationships, and having a sense of purpose in life are all of course, tremendously helpful to the healing process as well. Making improvements in your diet however, is usually the first step necessary before a person is able to implement these other elements.

For example, it's difficult to exercise when you have no energy, or to enjoy loving relationships when you're sick, tired, and irritable. As you start improving the quality of your diet, you will start feeling better, and other areas of your life will start improving as a result. Health is your natural state of being. If you want to restore it or prevent it from being lost, pay particular attention to this final universal guideline: *account for ailments when making wise food choices*.

There isn't any condition in the body that can't be improved by improving your diet!

diet & *dis*-ease

There are three primary recommendations to consider when accounting for ailments when making wise food choices. Each plays an important role in the relationship between diet and *dis*-ease. These three primary recommendations are:

1 ~ follow the eating-for-health guidelines

First, you will want to follow the first four guidelines to fully support your body in functioning optimally. Often, this is enough to completely clear a condition. I can't tell you how many clients I have had who eliminated chemically-processed pseudofoods from their diets and haven't had symptoms since, including severe conditions such as seizures, migraines, and asthma attacks. Equally as many others have identified and eliminated their food sensitivities or freed themselves from an addictive stimulant and likewise, have become symptom-free.

It may take some time and detective work, but by eliminating these foods, even if they're not directly related to your specific affliction, you are creating an internal healing environment that will give your body a chance to work its magic. When the body is out of balance and *dis*-eased, one food is usually not to blame, but the array of foods that make up a poor eating lifestyle. As you improve your diet, you will experience a concurrent improvement in your overall health.

2 ~ eliminate and include specific foods to address specific conditions

In addition to adopting the other guidelines, you'll also want to hone in on specific foods that may be exacerbating your condition, as well as those that can aid in the healing process. For example, if you have kidney or gallstones, you may want to stay away from spinach, which is high in oxalic acid and can contribute to these problems. At the same time you could incorporate a lot of apples and pears and their juices in your diet as they are known to help dissolve the stones.

In the natural healthcare realm, arthritis is known as the "junk food" disease. Consequently, people who suffer from arthritis would do well to improve the overall quality of their diets in general. In specific, they could also benefit from avoiding vegetables in the nightshade family, including tomatoes, eggplant, potatoes, and chili peppers, which are known to exacerbate arthritic conditions.

In many cases children with ADD, ADHD, or autism have cleared these conditions completely just by going off fake foods, sugar and the common food allergens, and supplementing their diets with cod liver oil and green-food supplements. Similarly, people who have chronic sinus or bronchial congestion have cut out wheat and dairy products, the two most notorious mucous-producing foods, and are now able to breathe freely. Sugar, soy, and oranges are also known to produce mucous and should be avoided by people who are congested as well.

This is just a sampling of the many specific considerations to be taken into account. It's not the focus of this article to offer specific recommendations for individual maladies as that would encompass an entire volume. For more information, you may want to consult a whole foods nutritional consultant who is familiar with your particular malady, or do some research on your own. There are also some great books that list multiple conditions and nutritional recommendations, such as:

The closer a food is to its whole, fresh, natural state, the higher its nutritional value.

- *How to Get Well*, by Paavo Airola
- *Foods for Health & Healing*, by Yogi Bhajan
- *Healing with Whole Foods*, by Paul Pitchford
- *Healthy Healing*, by Linda Page
- *Prescription for Nutritional Healing*, by James & Phyllis Balch
- *Eating Alive: Prevention Thru Good Digestion*, by Dr. Jonn Matsen, N.D.
- *Food is Your Best Medicine*, by Dr. Henry Bieler

And other books entirely devoted to specific ailments or systems, such as:

- *How to Eat Away Arthritis*, by Lauri Aesoph
- *Preventing & Reversing Arthritis Naturally*, by Raquel Martin
- *The Yeast Connection*, by Dr. William Crook
- *Sinus Survival*, by Robert S. Ivker & Todd H. Nelson

There are many other books available on the market today. Peruse the bookstore to find what will help *you*.

3 ~ cleanse, clear, & rejuvenate your system

Finally, you will want to take into consideration that symptoms are often the mere tip of the iceberg to an underlying body-mind system that is weakened, congested, and out of balance. This *dis*-eased internal environment frequently requires more than a change in your daily diet to bring it back to a state of health and well-being.

The road to good health is paved with good intestines—and liver, and kidneys, and stomach, and spleen, and all other internal organs. Cleansing, clearing, and rejuvenating the organs and systems of the body are usually necessary to restore balance, strength, and optimal function. There are a variety of ways to do this, from mono-diets to juice fasting, to herbal teas and remedies. Once again, volumes have been written on the topic of cleansing. The *Basic Elimination Diet* outlined in the previous section and upcoming articles in this section are a great place to start.

Cleansing your system is also a great maintenance and preventative strategy. If you're not currently suffering from any particular symptoms or ailments, remember that if you don't spend time and money on health now, be prepared to spend time and money on sickness later. And if you do find yourself in a state of symptomatic *dis*-ease, remember: *there isn't any condition in the body that can't be improved by improving your diet*!

quote: *There is little the doctor can do to overcome what the patient will not.*

—Dr. Mark Percival

No-Nonsense Nutrition

Article Series ~ By Kelly Hayford, CNC, Author *If It's Not Food, Don't Eat It!*

Finding Your Natural Weight

quote: *I think we place too much emphasis upon the weight loss issue and too little emphasis upon health and wellness for the mind, the body and the spirit.*

— Dr. Pamela Peeke

Maria was 280 pounds when she began an *Eating-for-Health* teleprogram. When I spoke with her five months later, she had lost 50 pounds at an average rate of ten pounds per month. But what was most heartwarming to hear was what she told the group during the final class of the program.

"I have done a zillion different diets throughout my life, and obviously gained it all back every time," Maria shared. "But for the first time in my life I feel like what I have learned I can actually do for the rest of my life. For the first time I feel really hopeful about being able to keep the weight off, because I'm not on a diet. Instead I am developing an eating lifestyle that I can live with for the long haul."

Maria focused on implementing the first two *Eating-for-Health Guidelines*. She switched from pseudofood brands to natural food brands, and started eating nothing sweeter than fruit, except on special occasions such as her birthday and Easter. She was enjoying the new foods she was discovering and no longer craved sweets. In fact, when her birthday came around, she was pleasantly surprised to find that she didn't even want the cake and ice cream she used to live for!

Don't underestimate the power of the *Eating-for-Health Guidelines*. People get obsessed with their weight and go in search of special weight loss diets and products to no avail. Instead, get obsessed with your health and creating an *Eating-for-Health lifestyle* you can live with. Your weight will take care of itself as Maria's story illustrates. There are however, a few specific tidbits worth knowing.

things to consider in finding your natural weight

1 ~ Strategies focused on losing weight conjure up the idea of eating less, hunger and deprivation, sometimes at the expense of overall good health and well-being. Although very common, this isn't the wisest approach and is often fleeting and unsuccessful in the long run. It's wiser to focus on finding your natural weight by restoring health and balance to your body, rather than losing weight. Many people believe that in order to lose weight they will have to deprive themselves of foods they love. This fear of loss alone can prevent them from achieving their goal. Start adding natural, healthy foods into your diet and put your focus on *gaining* these new additions into your diet rather than *losing* something.

2 ~ There are some things that are important to lose however, like foods that contain MSG and aspartame. In addition to the many other problems associated with MSG, it can also contribute to weight gain by causing those who eat it to crave foods. That's one of the reasons manufacturers put it in their products. It keeps you coming back for more! MSG is a neurotransmitter that affects the hunger and weight control centers of the brain. It's actually fed to laboratory animals to fatten them up for research without increasing their food intake.

There isn't any condition in the body that can't be improved by improving your diet!

3 ~ Drinking just one soda or sweetened beverage per day can increase the risk for obesity in children by 60%, according to a study cited in the Lancet. Needless to say, reducing or eliminating your sweetened beverage consumption can be tremendously helpful in finding and maintaining your natural weight. But don't look to diet drinks that contain artificial sweeteners…

4 ~ Aspartame should also be avoided if you are trying to lose weight. Contrary to popular belief, there is nothing diet about these toxic sweeteners. Aspartame is addictive and causes people to crave junk foods, snack foods and more artificially-sweetened foods and beverages. There are many other adverse symptoms and conditions associated with aspartame as well, much like MSG. Educate yourself about this substance. It's not a food, it's a toxic chemical. For more information on this topic, read: *Excitotoxins: The Taste that Kills,* by Russell Blaylock.

5 ~ Another often little known factor that can interfere with the ability to lose weight has to do with food intolerances. It is vitally important to identify and clear food allergies and sensitivities. Many people have lost significant amounts of weight just by eliminating wheat or dairy from their diet, for example. *Section 4* has everything you need to go on a *Basic Elimination Diet* to help you identify food sensitivities. It will also help you lose weight.

6 ~ There is a lot of hoopla about eating a low-fat or no-fat diet these days which is frankly, just silly. Our bodies need fat to function. The 'good' fats that is. The real problem is that people are eating mostly 'bad' fats and not getting any 'good' fats. Not getting the essential fats your body needs compromises every function in the body, including digestion and elimination, hormonal balance and production, brain function, the immune system, even metabolism. Switch to a 'no-*bad*-fat' and 'adequate-good-fat' diet and your health will increase while your weight decreases.

7 ~ High-protein diets are equally as silly. Sure you can lose weight, but often only temporarily, and also at the risk of your overall health. Balance, combined with persistence, and patience are always the key to establishing and maintaining your natural weight.
If you eat anything in excess, make it fresh vegetables!

8 ~ Stevia is a natural sweetener that actually helps you lose weight by reducing cravings for sweet and fatty foods. It also improves digestion which is important in reducing excess weight. (See *Section 3: Natural Sweeteners* for more on the benefits of stevia.)

9 ~ Cleansing and clearing your internal environment is an important part of any healthcare regime, and that includes restoring and maintaining normal weight. Detoxifying the organs and systems of the body will help improve digestion and elimination, reduce food cravings, and increase metabolism, all of which add up to a trimmer, healthier, more energetic body. The *Basic Elimination Diet* is a moderate cleanse and a great place to start.

factoid: *If you strive for thin, you'll never win. Strive for health and thin will follow.*

— Elson Haas, M.D.

Improving Digestion & Elimination

No-Nonsense Nutrition

Article Series ~ By Kelly Hayford, CNC, Author *If It's Not Food, Don't Eat It!*

Section 5, No. 3

Copyright 2008
Kelly Hayford

quote: *Today, as in no other period in the history of mankind, we have more problems with the intestinal tract -- the colon, the small intestine, along with the rest of the digestive system, causing a generation of degenerative diseases. We suffer from a multitude of colon and digestive ailments...a direst cause of many of the diseases of mankind.*

— Stan Malstrom, N.D.

It seems almost every other network television commercial is for either a pharmaceutical drug or over-the-counter remedy for one sort of digestive or eliminative problem or another—fiber solutions, laxatives, *Bean-o*, drugs for acid reflux, etc. This speaks to the widespread problems we're currently experiencing with these vital body functions at a cultural level.

Interestingly, many of the commercials in-between are for the poor-quality processed, fake foods that caused these problems in the first place! I have to laugh whenever I see a commercial advertising tantalizing mega-portions of some kind of digestively nightmarish food—the mere sight of which could induce a belch or two—followed by another commercial for the latest heartburn medication.

But poor digestion and elimination are no laughing matter. In fact, they can be the cause of much more than the acute discomforts and embarrassment we readily associate with them. In addition to the more obvious chronic disorders such as irritable bowel syndrome, acid reflux, Crohn's disease and colon cancer, what many people don't realize is that a weakened, ailing digestive and eliminative system can also be causing sinus problems, allergies, arthritis, depression, recurrent colds and flu, headaches, fatigue, and other menacing *dis*-eases of the body.

Optimal digestion and elimination are key to overall good health. In order to achieve optimal digestive and eliminative function on a regular basis, it's paramount to follow the *Eating-for-Health Guidelines* and *Healthy Habits* on a regular basis. Following are some other considerations you should know that can help.

it all begins with digestion

Most people have a deficiency of vitamins, minerals, and enzymes because they don't eat enough fresh, raw fruits and vegetables. The fresher food is the more alive it is, which means the more enzymes and life-force energy it contains. Enzymes are not only contained in fresh, living (raw) foods, but also produced in the body. The combination of the two sources of enzymes work together for proper digestion, assimilation, and elimination of the foods you eat.

Unfortunately, most Americans eat very little fresh, living food. Consequently, their body's digestive enzyme stores are exhausted from consuming an excessive amount of cooked or processed (dead) food, which requires double or more enzyme activity to make up for those provided for by fresh, enzyme-rich foods.

Most people could benefit from eating more raw foods. The problem is, because most have been raised on overly-processed and primarily cooked foods and little to no raw foods, their weakened systems are often not accustomed to digesting and eliminating raw foods. This is evidenced by the abdominal discomfort, gas, bloating, and disturbed bowel function that those who fit this profile sometimes experience upon introducing raw foods into their diet.

If this is the case for you, start with easy-to-digest, steamed vegetables (i.e. zucchini, carrots, etc.) and gradually integrate more raw foods and more difficult to digest vegetables (i.e. broccoli, cauli-flower, etc.) into your diet over time. In addition, eating big plates of many digestively incompatible foods at one sitting is very disruptive to the digestive system. Keep it simple and follow the food combining tips as outlined in the *Healthy Habits*.

My favorite book that can help you further with this topic is *Eating Alive: Prevention Thru Good Digestion,* by Jonn Matsen, N.D. It is a fabulous book that will completely change the way you think about food and how your digestion, elimination and overall body works. Read this humorous, yet informative book. Like many others, you'll be glad you did.

troubleshooting elimination

People frequently approach chronic constipation, diarrhea or other elimination problems by resorting to laxatives, colon cleansers or anti-diarrhea medications for assistance, treating these challenges in isolation of the digestive function. While this may be advisable in acute cases as temporary assistance to get things back on track, it's important to remember that elimination is the latter part of the digestive process. Everything you do on a regular basis leading up to the elimination event is what's most important. If you should find yourself in a position of having troubles in this area however, it's wise to address them as soon as possible in order to get your system in order.

To do this, go off foods that may be slowing things down (i.e. foods to which you may be sensitive such as dairy, wheat, sugar, fried foods, etc.). If things are really backed up, consider taking some herbal cleansing formulas. Drinking ginger or other herbal teas is helpful as well. You may also consider irrigating the colon by doing an enema or having a colonic. Colon irrigation is a time-honored way of cleansing the body and restoring health to a clogged system. Going on a *Basic Elimination Diet*, eating minimally, or drinking only liquids (broths, herbal teas, etc.) until the colon clears will help too. Whatever you do, *don't* allow the waste to continue to back up.

Diarrhea often alternates with being constipated. Essentially both conditions are sending the same message: *what you're eating or doing in your life, especially poor eating and stressful living, are not work-*

ing for you. Definitely make use of temporary measures, but ultimately adopt new habits that will eliminate the cause.

My two favorite books for learning more about the colon and optimal elimination are *The Colon Health Handbook*, by Robert Gray and *Dr. Jensen's Guide to Better Bowel Care: A Complete Program for Tissue Cleansing Through Bowel Management*, by Dr. Bernard Jensen.

No-Nonsense Nutrition

Article Series ~ By Kelly Hayford, CNC, Author If It's Not Food, Don't Eat It!

Cleanse & Clear Your System
For Optimal Health, Energy & *Dis*-ease Prevention

factoid: *The colon is a sewage system, but by neglect and abuse it becomes a cesspool. When it is clean and normal we are well and happy; but let it stagnate and it will distill the poisons of decay, fermentation and putrefaction into the blood, poisoning the brain and the nervous system so it will become mentally depressed and irritable; it will poison the lungs so the breath is foul, poison the digestive organs so we are distressed and bloated; and poison the blood so the skin is sallow and unhealthy.*

— Dr. William Hunter

After doing a cleanse, drinking only juices for a few days, I woke up one morning with an odd yet distantly familiar taste in my mouth. It was very distinctive, sort of metallic, and I racked my brain throughout the day as it stayed with me to figure out where I had encountered it before. It finally came to me.

It was the same taste I had had in my mouth for the duration of the ten days that I took copious amounts of a potent antibiotic when I was in the Peace Corps some 15 years before. I had always heard that people release toxins and drugs that have been stored in the organs and tissues when they fast or cleanse, and had always felt this to be true when I had done a cleanse. But this was the first time I had a directly identifiable experience of this.

It's a long-held notion among natural health advocates that toxins and chemicals can be stored in the tissues and organs of the body, wreaking havoc with your health. In recent years scientific evidence has proven this historically held theory to be valid. In a recent PBS program, Bill Moyers took a blood test that revealed he had numerous toxic chemicals in his system, including heavy metals, DDT, and other harmful substances. This blood test only accounted for environmental pollutants, however, and did not even include all the toxic chemicals that are ingested from eating processed pseudofood.

Toxins from your natural metabolic processes can also accumulate in the body if it is so overloaded and weakened that it is rendered incapable of performing its rudimentary detoxification process. This is very common in our culture with its poor-eating and lifestyle habits and the added burden of environmental toxins and consumption of large quantities of chemicals in the form of over-the-counter and pharmaceutical drugs. For this reason, it is a wise practice to cleanse and rejuvenate the body on a regular basis.

In addition to helping clear food cravings and addictions, cleansing is especially in order for those who want to prevent the onset of, or are already experiencing, any kind of chronic health condition including arthritis, allergies, sinus trouble, digestive and eliminative problems, skin problems, excess weight and more.

an age-old concept
Cleansing is an age-old concept for restoring health, energy, strength, and balance

to the body-mind system that we have unfortunately, lost sight of in our modern, medically-oriented society. Cleansing benefits every cell, tissue, organ, and system of the body by releasing stored waste and toxins, giving your bodily functions a rest, and improving digestion, assimilation, and elimination. As a result of cleansing, your body chemistry will inevitably change and you will lose the desire for health-robbing addictive foods and stimulants as balance is restored and the cycle of addiction is broken.

To understand the concept of cleansing, think of your kitchen garbage disposal. If you're using it properly, you feed only enough food into it that it can easily grind and process. If, instead, you keep shoving food into it beyond its capacity to process it, what will happen? First it will slow down, then it may get stuck, and finally it will stop working altogether. So, the garbage will just keep piling up.

The same thing happens with your digestive and eliminative system. If you keep shoveling food into it beyond its capacity to adequately digest and eliminate it, more than just your digestive system will start slowing down. You'll also have reduced energy, lowered immune function and will eventually develop a host of other maladies as well. This is especially true when you are shoveling in fake food that your system isn't equipped to process in the first place.

Even if you started eating absolutely pristinely today, you still have all the accumulated waste and chemical imbalances from yesterday to deal with. Just changing your diet and lifestyle will rectify much of this, but that will take consistent action over time and can sometimes take longer than most people want to wait; and some of it can only be released or brought into balance through an internal cleansing program designed to do the job. When you're not getting the results you want, as quickly as you want, the probability for being pulled back into old habits and addictions runs high. And this is where cleansing your internal environment can be a life-saver.

constant craving

Cleansing your system is a very effective, often necessary tool for breaking the cycle of cravings and addictions to unwanted foods and making the transition to a healthier eating lifestyle. Accumulated toxins and wastes in the liver/gallbladder, kidneys, colon, and other organs and tissues of the body create a highly acidic, polluted internal environment. So what does this have to do with cravings for stimulants and poor quality foods?

Although there are multiple factors at play, there are two primary factors that cause people with weakened, congested systems to crave certain foods. First, characteristic of a toxic inner environment is an overgrowth of yeasts, fungi, bacteria, viruses, parasites and worms. These yeastie beasties and other critters thrive on sugars and alcohol in their many forms. This can cause uncontrollable cravings for these substances as these buggers beg to be fed.

In addition, many people crave common food allergens such as wheat, dairy (pasteurized), corn and soy products. These foods are difficult to digest, especially for those with a weakened, congested digestive and eliminative tract. If you are not able to properly digest these foods, they sit in your gut fermenting and putrefying, which further proliferates the growth of harmful microorganisms. This causes you to crave more of these foods as once again, the critters they proliferate thrive on them.

So how can you reverse this internal state of affairs that may be causing chronic, irrepressible urges for a variety of unhealthy foods?

There isn't any condition in the body that can't be improved by improving your diet!

where to start

There are many different ways to cleanse the body, including herbal formulas, mono-diets, juice fasting, the Master cleanse (water and lemon juice fast), and colon irrigation. Often these different modalities are combined and are either geared to a general cleansing of the system, or to target specific organs or systems of the body such as the colon, liver/gallbladder, or urinary tract.

There are also cleansing protocols designed to address specific conditions such as yeast overgrowth (candida) or parasitic infestations. These two particular conditions often show up together and are both major culprits when it comes to food cravings and sensitivities.

Although there are many approaches, any approach must incorporate a basic elimination diet and a supplement protocol *for an adequate amount of time* in order to be successful. What constitutes an adequate amount of time will vary from person to person based on several factors including age, weight, constitution and severity of symptoms.

The best place for anyone to start when it comes to cleansing is also the best method for identifying and clearing food cravings and sensitivities: the *Basic Elimination Diet*. An elimination diet is also a wonderful tool to use in combination with many other kinds of cleansing, such as colonics, bowel cleanses or liver flushes, as it will enhance and accelerate the overall cleansing and healing process. A stand-alone basic elimination diet, however, is your best friend for breaking the cycle of cravings and addictions and identifying those foods to which you may be sensitive. It will also free up the digestive system so more energy is available for healing.

In a nutshell, a *Basic Elimination Diet* involves eliminating all stimulants and common food allergens from your diet for a designated amount of time. To help identify food intolerances, common food allergens may then be systematically re-introduced into the diet one at a time. For detailed instructions see *Section 5*.

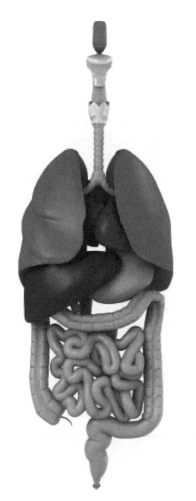

While an elimination diet has a mild to moderate cleansing affect, it is usually not enough. A protocol that includes high-quality herbal formulas and nutritional supplements is also imperative to truly detoxify and restore balance to your system.

Keep in mind that optimizing digestion, cleansing the colon and maintaining 2-3 bowel movements per day is essential before starting to cleanse parasites, candida and the deeper organs of elimination such as the liver/gallbladder. For these reasons, a colon cleansing product or protocol is essential for most people throughout any detoxification program.

It is also important to alkalize your system and restore the friendly bacteria with a quality probiotic (the good bacteria). For best results, consult with your natural healthcare practitioner for individual recommendations and an overall plan of action.

colon hydrotherapy

One method of cleansing that has recently been gaining in popularity is colon irrigation or colon hydrotherapy, which has been

The closer a food is to its whole, fresh, natural state, the higher its nutritional value.

used as a part of healing protocols in cultures throughout the world since ancient times. Modern day colonics are the quickest, least troublesome, most effective method I know of for cleansing and restoring balance to an ailing body-mind. I highly recommend a series of colonics for anyone who is suffering from chronic conditions and wants to jumpstart or accelerate the healing process.

You can eat the best diet in the world and take herbs and supplements from here until the cows come home, but if you don't clear out all the accumulated waste in your system you'll never get better. There are certain physical conditions that prevent some people from having them and there are also different colonic systems to choose from, depending on what is appropriate for you. Consult with a qualified colon hydrotherapist to learn more and see if colonics are right for you.

cleanse regularly

Some kind of cleansing is something you'll want to do regularly. It's like your closet or your garage. Stuff is always coming in and you have to clear it out one way or another. For this reason, it's wise to do an elimination diet or some other form of cleansing or combination periodically. Doing a cleanse at the beginning of each season, or one or two days a month, for example, is a long-time tradition for many.

Health is like a bank account. You can't continue to draw on it without making deposits. Going on an elimination diet or other kind of cleansing protocol is the equivalent of making a sizeable deposit. And the more you cleanse regularly, the less problems you will encounter.

Remember that cleansing is not an event, it's a process; a process that can take time and commitment. It's a process well worth the effort, however. Not only will your cravings for health-robbing, weight-inducing foods disappear, but you'll also enjoy more energy, clearer thinking and general well-being as a result.

quote: *Most people today are so toxic that fasting stirs old toxins up far faster than their already-- overloaded elimination organs can handle. Feeling worse is often the result.*
— Jon Matsen, N.D., *Eating Alive*

what to expect

Although many people feel better right away, it's important to understand that when you start cleansing you may feel worse before you feel better. This a natural part of the healing process as the body releases stored waste and restores balance. Symptoms may include headaches, fever, sinus drainage, skin break outs, constipation, diarrhea, fatigue, weakness, nervousness, irritability, negativity or depression, frequent urination, etc. The majority of reactions are tolerable and easy to endure. You may also be simultaneously noticing many improvements which will help.

Symptoms will vary according to the materials being discarded, the condition of your organs, and the amount of energy available. Generally speaking, the worse your diet and state of health prior to cleansing, the more symptoms you may have. The more you rest and sleep, the milder the symptoms will be and the sooner they'll subside. Most usually don't last more than a week.

If symptoms persist or are severe, consult with your healthcare practitioner and scale back on the protocol you are following. You might also get some relief from a colonic or by giving yourself an enema to help move things out of your system quicker (see next article for instructions). Most importantly, remember that improved health and energy await you on the other side!

No-Nonsense Nutrition

Article Series ~ By Kelly Hayford, CNC, Author *If It's Not Food, Don't Eat It!*

Section 5, No. 5

Copyright 2008
Kelly Hayford

Enema Instructions
How to Perform At-Home Colon Irrigation

Enemas are a therapeutic tool used throughout the ages to assist the colon in clearing unwanted material, thus expediting the bodies natural abilities to heal and repair. Doing a filtered water or wheat grass enema is also an effective way to get immediate relief from constipation, headaches, gas, bloating, and even assist with colds and flu. Enemas should be administered only on occasion, however, and not used as a substitute for healthy bowel movements.

plain water cleansing enema

A plain water enema can be used on its own or in preparation for a retention enema, such as the wheat grass enema described next. A few drops (10-12) of 100% pure tea tree oil or the juice of a fresh lemon can be added to the water to increase the cleansing effect.

supplies:

2 quart enema bag available at any drugstore
2 quarts *filtered* water (do not use tap water, it has chlorine and other toxins)
3 towels
privacy, if available!

directions:

1 ~ To make just the right temperature for the body, boil 2 cups water, fill enema bag about half way with room temperature water, add the boiling water, then fill the rest of the bag with room temperature water.

2 ~ Prepare bathroom by placing spreading one towel on the floor, preferably over a comfortable bath rug and fold the other two towels for under your hips.

3 ~ Hook the enema bag 2-4 feet above floor on a towel rack or door knob.

4 ~ Lie on back with hips on folded towels so hips are higher than head.

5 ~ Before inserting, release clamp to allow water to run through and force air out from the tube (very important, so air is not being forced into your colon!). Close clamp. Lubricate end of rectal insert with pure, unscented oil. Olive oil or castor oil are good choices. Insert tip into rectum.

6 ~ Slowly release clamp and allow water to flow into rectum. If you feel the need to release, get up and go!

7 ~ When bag is empty or no more fluid can be held, remove tip. Breathe and relax as much as possible during the process. Some people will need to release a few times before they reach the end of the bag, while others will be able to take in the whole bag.

8 ~ Repeat until water runs clear when you release.

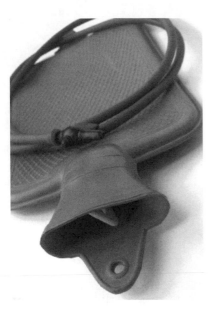

wheat grass enemas

Wheat grass is very high in magnesium and it pulls fat and other debris from the tissues. It also dilates the bile ducts and stimulates the liver, gallbladder and colon to purge unwanted material—even more so than coffee enemas in my experience. Another advantage is that the wheat grass puts nutrients *into* the body, rather than possibly depleting them as can be the case with coffee enemas.

If you can do fresh wheat grass juice, that is best. However, Green Kamut® powder which is the most convenient way to go and still very effective. Green Kamut® is a species of wheat grass available in powder and capsule form at most health food stores and online. It is also great to take internally on a regular basis to help alkalize your system. Follow these instructions for a fresh or powdered wheat grass enema:

ingredients

2-8 oz. fresh wheat grass juice
OR 2-8 heaping tsps. Green Kamut® powder
(start with 1-2 oz. and work up to using more in subsequent enemas as body acclimates)
2 quarts filtered water

directions

1 ~ First do cleansing enema with plain filtered water to clear colon. Usually 1-2 bags will do the trick. Adding 2 cups boiling water to the bag will make it the perfect temperature.

2 ~ Fill enema bag with water and wheat grass or Green Kamut® powder.

3 ~ Hook about 2-4 feet above floor (on towel rack or door knob) .

4 ~ Lie on your back with hips on folded towels to bring hips higher than head.

5 ~ Insert nozzle tip into rectum, using lubricant on tip (olive oil is a good choice).

6 ~ Slowly empty mixture into rectum, and hold inside rectum as long as possible. About 20-30 minutes is good. (When you first do a wheat grass enema you'll probably have to expel very hurriedly. Let it go! This is normal. The more you do them the easier they become to hold.)

7 ~ When bag is empty or no more fluid can be held, remove tip. Lie on each side for 5 minutes, while massaging abdomen if you can. Otherwise remain on your back, breathe and relax as much as possible.

8 ~ Empty contents of rectum into toilet.

9 ~ Repeat until bag is empty

Doing a series of Green Kamut® or fresh wheat grass enemas (one a day or every other day) in combination with a cleansing diet is a great internal cleanse. At the Hippocrates Institute they do wheat grass enemas up to 3x day for cancer patients or very sick individuals.

For more on wheat grass and wheat grass enemas, read: *The Wheat Grass Book*, by Ann Wigmore.

No-Nonsense Nutrition

Article Series ~ By Kelly Hayford, CNC, Author *If It's Not Food, Don't Eat It!*

Cold & Flu Busters
Staying Well All Year Round

It's easier to prevent *dis*-ease than it is to reverse it. Which means ongoing preventative self care is the best strategy for avoiding colds and flu—not to mention a host of other chronic and acute *dis*-eases. Contrary to popular belief, the germ theory is only part of the equation. The biggest cause of colds and flu is an unhealthy, weakened body-mind system that serves as a friendly host for bacteria and viruses. Practice the following on a regular basis to keep healthy and strong. And turn to the next page for tips on how to avoid or get rid of an unwanted bug.

adequately nourish your body
eat whole, fresh, natural—REAL foods 70-100% of the time...
~ *Fresh, preferably organic fruits & vegetables*
~ *Whole grains—brown rice, oats, millet, quinoa*
~ *Legumes—white beans, red beans, mung beans, aduki beans, etc.*
~ *Fresh, preferably organic meats, fish & poultry*

make sure you're getting enough fiber...
~ *Eat a high-fiber diet as described above.*
~ *Supplement with a mixture of quality fibers such as flax meal, apple pectin, oat bran and psyllium. (Note: psyllium by itself may clog the colon.)*

make sure you're getting enough of the "good fats"...
~ *Consume 1-3 tbsps. beneficial fats daily, such as extra virgin olive oil, sesame oil, virgin coconut oil and/or raw, unsalted nuts and seeds*
~ *Take an essential fatty acids daily (Evening Primrose oil, fish oils, etc.)*
~ *Avoid the "bad fats" such as hydrogenated oils and fried foods*
~ *Take Juice Plus+® daily -- whole food based nutrition, including juice powder concentrates from 17 different fruits, vegetables and grains. (See How to Choose a Whole Food Supplement.)*

keep your body clear & strong

* Exercise regularly
* Get plenty of rest
* Drink plenty of purified water
* Minimize stress & overwhelm
* Maintain balanced blood sugar
* Alkalize your internal environment
* Optimize your digestion
* Keep your bowels moving!

at the first sign of symptoms

How you respond to "something coming on" is crucial. At the first hint of symptoms cancel all non-priority appointments and get horizontal ASAP. If you don't take yourself down your body will do it for you! Eliminate all sweets, alcohol and caffeine as they deplete immune function. Immediately start taking a cold and flu busting formula. Experiment to find what works best for you. My favorites include:

~ *Cold Snap,* by OHCO Herbal Co.

~ *Inner Defense or Thieves,* by Young Living Essential Oils

~ *Wellness Formula Herbal Defense Complex & Wellness Herbal Resistance Liquid,* both by Source Naturals

~ *Oscillococcinum,* by Boiron

~ *Echinacea/Goldenseal,* by Zand Herbals

when you fall victim

The emotional factor associated with colds & flu is overwhelm. Now that you've actually succumbed you'll want to cancel *all* appointments, turn off your phone and SLEEP & REST as much as possible. Increase the amount and frequency of your cold and flu busting formula, follow the specific dietary recommendations to the right and consider these tips for specific conditions:

for aches & pains and general symptomatic relief...

~ *Draw a hot bath. Add Bragg's apple cider vinegar and Epsom salt, 1 cup per 100 lbs of body weight. Scrub skin gently and soak for at least 20 minutes.*

for upper respiratory conditions...

~ *Breathe Deep Tea,* by Traditional Medicinals

~ *Osha tincture or herbal blend that contains osha*

for sore throat...

~ *Gargle with diluted grapefruit seed extract*

~ *Throat Coat Tea,* by Celestial Seasonings

for congested or runny sinuses...

~ *Flush sinuses with therapeutic solution using a neti pot (see photo)*

~ *Run a cool-mist humidifier or vaporizer day & night*

avoid recurrence

Take a maintenance dose of your cold & flu buster formula. Ease into your regular routine *gradually.* Double your dose of Juice Plus+® for a few weeks to boost your immune system.

---

cold & flu buster's
Dietary Recommendations

in general
Eat easy to digest foods such as homemade soups & broths, steamed veggies & brown rice.

in specific
Eliminate immune depleters & mucous producers...
- sugar & sweets
- orange juice!
- common food allergens - especially wheat & dairy

Eat plenty immune boosters...
- green peppers
- chili peppers
- cayenne & curry spices
- onions, garlic, ginger

Drink plenty of...
- purified WATER
- herbal teas
- diluted fresh lemon juice

fyi...

Avoid taking antibiotics — they destroy beneficial intestinal flora & create resistant strains of bacteria and viruses — i.e. bigger, badder bugs that are even harder to get rid of!

No-Nonsense Nutrition

Article Series ~ By Kelly Hayford, CNC, Author *If It's Not Food, Don't Eat It!*

Emotional Eating:
An Often Misunderstood Phenomenon

quote: *...your mood (often created by the foods you choose) determines what you eat at your next meal. Imbalanced eating habits trigger a vicious cycle where you feel worse and worse and turn repeatedly to the wrong foods for a quick fix....In contrast, when you make the right food choices, you're providing fuel for a healthy body, a good mood, an active mind, and a high energy level.*

—Elizabeth Somer, *Food & Mood*

The concept of *emotional eating* is most often based on the notion that people become emotionally upset, which then leads them to binge on large quantities of primarily low-quality junk foods as a source of comfort. What is seldom discussed however, is what triggered the emotional upset and cravings for certain foods in the first place. It begs the age-old question: *which came first, the chicken or the egg?* Or in this case: *which came first, the emotional upset or poor nutrition and junk-food binging?*

This is an important distinction. Negative emotions don't just spring out of nowhere. Improper nutrition is a primary *cause* of imbalanced psychological states and frequently triggers emotional upset, which in turn perpetuates the cycle of imbalanced eating and imbalanced emotional states. The only way to loop out of this vicious cycle is to balance the body's internal chemistry by providing adequate nutrients and eliminating the offending foods.

The fact that food has a tremendous influence on how you think and feel is frequently ignored, diminished or unknown. Whether it be chronic depression, irritability, anxiety, fear, anger, obsessive thinking, or constant worrying, the *Standard American Diet* is loaded with foods that not only cause physical imbalance and deterioration, but mental and emotional imbalance and deterioration as well.

At the same time, the *Standard American Diet* is lacking in the whole, fresh, natural foods loaded with the vital nutrients needed for proper brain function and mental health. Having an awareness and understanding of this can significantly increase your ability to decipher which foods are best for you, and can also significantly increase your chances for successfully changing your eating habits.

As people begin to eat healthier and develop more body awareness, they're frequently amazed to discover that more often than not, poor eating in general and certain foods in particular trigger emotional upsets that cause them to unconsciously eat more of the offending foods rather than the other way around. And in fact, the healthier and more balanced they eat, the healthier and more balanced their mental and emotional states become. Because normal brain function has been restored, they no longer react to situations as they would have in the past. They find they're able to maintain a balanced state of emotional well-being as long as they maintain their healthy eating lifestyle.

Section 5, No. 7

Copyright 2008
Kelly Hayford

it's also about what you *don't* eat

As you make the change to a healthier eating lifestyle, remember that proper nutrition is as much about the foods you eat as it is about those you *don't* eat. Foods to which you are sensitive or allergic, including the common food allergens, processed foods with chemical additives, especially aspartame and MSG, and extreme foods such as sugar and caffeine, are all major culprits in creating a psychological environment ripe for emotional fragility and overreacting to situations you might otherwise let slide.

Equally problematic are the nutritional deficiencies that can result from the absence of nutrient-rich foods in your diet. In other words, it's as important to identify and eliminate poor quality offensive foods, as it is to be sure you're getting high-quality nutritious foods and adequate amounts of the basic nutrients such as green foods and essential fatty acids. Following the *Eating-for-Health Guidelines* and the *Dietary Basics*, in combination with heeding the messages of your body, will help you determine how best to accomplish this in accordance with your body's particular needs.

become a detective

Whether someone is emotionally binging or experiencing acute, chronic, or intermittent irritability, depression, anxiety, hypersensitivity, fear, anger, worry or any other disagreeable emotional state, learning to listen to the body and correctly interpret and respond to the messages it sends is a worthwhile skill for everyone to develop. The best way to do this is to become a detective.

Keeping a written or mental journal of what you're eating and any corresponding physical or psychological symptoms is one way of playing detective with yourself. Another way, and probably the most effective, is to train yourself to investigate situations in the moment, and at the same time take immediate action to remedy the current situation and reflect on how to prevent yourself from repeating the causative behavior in the future.

To do this, take a moment whenever you're feeling out of sorts to stop and ask yourself:

1. *What exactly am I feeling both emotionally and physically (i.e., headache, fatigue, irritability, emotional sensitivity, anger, spaciness, etc.)?*

2. *When did I start feeling this way?*

3. *What foods or beverages have I had, or not had, today or yesterday that may have caused or contributed to this imbalanced state?*

4. *What foods or beverages do I regularly have or not have, that may be causing an overall state of imbalance in my body and mind?*

5. *What actions can I take at this moment to start feeling better and get my body and mind back into a balanced state of well-being?*

6. *What actions can I take to help prevent this from happening in the future?*

It may take some time to get to know what your body is trying to tell you. Keep playing detective. It will help accelerate the process. The more aware you become of what precipitates symptoms and reactions, the better you'll be able to make corrections. In addition, as the specific associations between what you're eating and how you feel become clearer, the more motivated you'll be to eliminate the foods and habits that are causing the problems in the first place. The desire to feel good will soon override the desire for injurious foods.

section six

Make It So!
Tips for Making Eating for Health a Reality

No-Nonsense Nutrition

Article Series ~ By Kelly Hayford, CNC, Author *If It's Not Food, Don't Eat It!*

Kitchen Set Up & Food Shopping Tips

Contrary to popular belief, eating an abundance of whole, fresh, natural foods has gotten even easier these days. Bagged carrots, broccoli slaw and salad greens, rice cookers, vacuum sealers, food processors and other kitchen gadgets can all help cut down on time spent in the kitchen.

For most people cutting processed foods out completely would be a major feat in our fast-paced world. Instead, focus on cutting out the chemical-laden pseudo-foods, then gradually reduce the percentage of time you eat natural brand processed foods, and all the while increase the percentage of whole, fresh, natural foods in your diet. This is a sure recipe for better health and more energy.

kitchen set up & equipment

In order to successfully integrate consuming an abundance of natural foods as a lifestyle habit and enjoy doing it, it is imperative to create a user-friendly kitchen. Doing so will greatly increase the likelihood of this sacred room being used more frequently for its intended purpose—the proper care and fueling of our human vehicles with nutritious foods.

Performing a clean sweep of all pseudofoods as described in *Section 1* is the perfect time to take inventory of what needs to be done. Whether you decide to make a clean sweep or not, there are three main elements of every kitchen that you will want to have in order.

1 ~ You'll want to be sure that all areas of the kitchen are well organized and free of clutter as much as possible. Throw out expired foods and kitchen gadgets that are broken or never get used. Organize what remains with like items in accordance with their frequency of use.

For example, place frequently used items close to the area in which they will be used and can be easily accessed, such as spices and hot mitts near the stove. Stow away fine China, the turkey roaster, and other *in*frequently used items in the more difficult to access places of the pantry, cupboards or even in a closet or storage place outside the kitchen. Place only those items you use regularly on the counter to free-up adequate space for unencumbered food preparation.

2 ~ Next, you'll want to be sure you have all the necessary kitchenware and equipment. A good set of pots and pans, including a vegetable steamer, a set of sharp knives, a cutting board and lots of hard plastic, or better yet, glass containers with lids for food storage and convenient take-along, are all essential.

There are many other items, such as a food processor, blender, grinder, juicer, rice cooker, crock-pot, vacuum sealer, and salad spinner that are also very helpful. Don't buy or keep things around that you don't need or will never use however, as they will only end up contributing to the clutter you

Section 6, No. 1

Copyright 2008
Kelly Hayford

are trying to reduce. Which equipment gets used will be different for everyone. Some people couldn't live without their food processor, while I personally would be lost without my juicer and vacuum sealer.

3 ~ But the only thing that will keep you from preparing homemade, nutritious foods more than a disorganized, ill-equipped kitchen is a kitchen that is lacking a supply of whole, fresh, natural ingredients to prepare. This is the final all-important element of a user-friendly kitchen oriented toward healthy eating. It must be regularly and adequately stocked with nutrient-rich, natural foods, which usually takes a little forethought.

shopping tips

Making a shopping list before you head to the store is always a good idea, and an absolute necessity when first starting to make changes in your diet. A well-executed shopping list is not only a valuable time-saver and stress-reducer, but will also keep your food choices on the right track.

Create a general list of staple goods that you'll want to keep on hand, but won't need to buy every week, such as baking supplies and condiments. Check this list and make note of anything you need on a weekly basis. You'll also want to keep a list of things you buy every week, such as produce, eggs, and bread. Finally, you'll want to include items that you don't buy regularly, but may need for special meals you're planning for that particular week. As for the actual shopping, the more routines you can establish the better.

Try to limit your trips to the store to 1-2 times per week, and establish specific days for food shopping, such as Monday for your major food shopping and Wednesday for fresh meats and a few extraneous items. Also, frequent the same stores as much as possible. Knowing where things are will save you time and reduce frustration. Following the same route each time you shop will similarly expedite the process, and can also jog your memory for any items you may have forgotten to include on your list.

When checking labels on natural-brand processed foods, remember that items are listed in descending order of ingredient concentrations. Also, hydrogenated oils, refined sweeteners, and ten syllable words you can't pronounce are all best left on the store shelf, even if you found them at the health food store.

Unfortunately, an increasing number of *un*natural food items have made their way into what used to be authentic natural foods stores. While scrutinizing labels may be necessary when first transitioning to new, healthier brands, sticking with those you like and have become familiar with will help minimize time spent on this task in the future.

Similarly, planning meals in advance will save you time, and make coming up with your weekly shopping list a breeze.

No-Nonsense Nutrition

Article Series ~ By Kelly Hayford, CNC, Author *If It's Not Food, Don't Eat It!*

Section 6, No. 2

Copyright 2008
Kelly Hayford

Menu Planning & Making Healthy Foods Available

Establishing a general plan for each day of the week makes overall menu planning quick and easy. For example, a general weekly plan for dinner might look something like this:

- *Monday* – fish
- *Tuesday* – chicken
- *Wednesday* – pasta
- *Thursday* – beans and rice
- *Friday* – natural brand frozen pizza or other entrée
- *Saturday* – eat out
- *Sunday* – special dinner

With a general notion of what's for dinner for a particular night of the week, you can easily plug in different dishes from week to week to create variety. Having halibut one week and salmon the next on Monday night, fish night, for instance. Set up your plan to suit your schedule and your lifestyle. When trying a new recipe, be sure to include all the ingredients on your upcoming weekly shopping list.

As for specifics, *Section 1* provides detailed descriptions of what to eat and how much depending on your individual needs. If you need more help and have long-wished that someone else could plan everything out for you, including a categorized shopping list, your wish has come true.

There is a fabulous service called *Menu-Mailer* now available online at a very reasonable cost. Visit their website for a free sample of a week's worth of menu plans and coordinating shopping list at www.MenuMailer.net. If you decide to subscribe to this service, a menu plan will be e-mailed to you directly each week. Because brand names are not listed, make sure to use only natural, additive-free brands, and organic produce and animal protein whenever possible.

maximize availability of healthy foods

It's times when we're the most hurried, stressed or hungry that lead us to resort to what are sometimes the worst possible food choices we can make. And we don't have to look too far to find them. To counter this situation, always have quick and easy-to-prepare foods of a healthier variety on hand that can be made up when there is no time to make something, or take along with you whenever you head out the door such as additive-free natural brand frozen and canned foods.

Although I don't generally recommend these kinds of foods because they're devoid of the vital life force and enzymes that give food its magical quality, if it comes down to a last minute choice between a natural-brand frozen dinner or can of soup and a stop at the fast-food drive-through, there's no doubt that the first choice would be your best.

Knowing that you have a quick can of soup or frozen entrée you can heat up in a matter of minutes can save you from having many a bad food day. Make up a fresh salad or side of fresh steamed vegetables, and you've got a quick and delicious meal that isn't half bad.

There are a variety of both canned and bottled all-natural soups to choose from, as well as a variety of additive-free frozen dinners. Check labels carefully. Unfortunately, there are a few brands that have made there way into the health foods stores that contain autolyzed yeast extract, which is a source of MSG.

Thai Kitchen also makes a great rice noodle soup that comes in little packets. Throw in some chopped carrots and zucchini to the boiling water and a tablespoon of virgin coconut oil and you have a satisfying gluten-free meal. Add a raw egg at the end and allow the heat of the water and noodles to cook it for added protein and satiation.

Also be sure to take advantage of the many pre-washed bagged salads, herbs, baby carrots and other chopped raw, veggies now available at grocery stores. Once again, check labels to be sure nothing has been added as a preservative, which is sometimes the case. Similarly, you'll want to keep plenty of raw fruit around for a sweet and easy snack. These ready-to-eat raw foods are the healthiest fast foods out there.

pack it in!

When you head out the door, be sure to pack it in! It's a junk-food jungle out there and you can never be sure if whole, fresh, natural foods will be available when going to work, school or social outings unless you bring it yourself. Because vending machines, convenience food stores and eating out can be very costly, you'll save money too!

One of the smartest things you can do is to bring a bag of the aforementioned grab-n-go foods with you at the beginning of the week and keep it in the refrigerator at work or school, if possible, for quick snacks and lunches all week. Because you don't want to be eating processed foods every day however, you can pack up leftovers from dinner the night before to take along too. Which leads us to the absolute number one guideline when it comes to making healthier foods available on a regular basis: *whenever you're cooking or otherwise preparing food, always make enough to put leftovers in serving-sized, sealable containers for the following day.*

Yes of course, the optimum way to go would be to make foods fresh just before you eat them, and if you can, by all means do so. But for most of us, it just isn't possible, and healthy leftovers are much better than many other choices you could make.

fast-food health food

In addition, preparing fresh vegetables in advance for use in a variety of meals and recipes will turn health food into fast food and further increase the likelihood that you will make healthier food choices regularly. It becomes a matter of just pulling things out of the fridge and heating them up or tossing them in a salad or quick recipe. More on this topic coming up next.

No-Nonsense Nutrition

Article Series ~ By Kelly Hayford, CNC, Author *If It's Not Food, Don't Eat It!*

Getting More Vegetables into Your Diet
Preparing a Week's Worth of Vegetables & Other Tips

factoid: *The latest dietary guidelines call for 5-13 servings of fruits and vegetables a day, depending on one's caloric intake.*

— Harvard School of Public Health

Vegetables are the only food group that *everybody* agrees we should be eating the most and yet, they are in fact, what we're eating the least.

Pain and fear are great motivators, however, so as the rates of chronic degenerative *dis*-eases have skyrocketed in the past few years, interest in eating healthier in general and eating more vegetables in specific, has started to rise as well. This is especially true as more and more studies roll out with concrete evidence that vegetables are one of the number one blockers to *dis*-ease of virtually every kind.

Less time in the kitchen, less knowledge of how to prepare them and consequently less desire and taste for them are all to blame for not eating our vegetables. There were many years when there was rarely a day that I had a vegetable. Today there isn't a day that goes by that I don't have four or five or six or more!

This is how it's supposed to be, and it can happen for you too. Just follow the upcoming three simple steps to always have an abundance of fresh vegetables on hand that are chopped and ready to go. Be sure to keep a stash of frozen vegetables—additive-free and organic whenever possible—on hand for back up.

preparing veggies in advance

Because fresh produce begins to lose its nutrients and start the oxidative process as soon as it is cut, it is best to chop vegetables right before cooking or eating them. That is the ideal scenario and if you have the time to do it, great. However, for most people this is not always practical and is one of the reasons why people don't eat enough vegetables. The mere thought of having to do all that preparation before each meal can be overwhelming.

For this reason, the best way to ensure that you're eating vegetables on a regular basis is to have them available and ready to throw in the steamer or add to your chosen recipe at any given time. This can easily be achieved by blocking out a 1-2 hour chunk of time once or twice a week in order to wash and chop vegetables, which can then be stored in the refrigerator for quick and easy access.

Adopting this process as a lifestyle habit may take some time, but it's one of the best things you can do for your health. Enrolling children, spouses, roommates or other household members to help can lessen the burden on any one person and make it an enjoyable family time together. You might also consider hiring someone to help as well. The teenager next door or in your own household is a good place to start. The first couple of times you shop and chop vegetables as described will take a little longer, but as you get more familiar with this process it will go much quicker, so have fun and persevere!

1 ~ shop

- To ensure freshness, plan to shop for produce the day of, or the day before you plan to chop and store it, whenever possible.

- Shop for produce that is locally grown, in-season, and organic whenever possible.

- Choose vegetables that are dark in color, firm to the touch and have no bruises or bad spots.

- For steaming, roasting, or grilling, choose zucchini, yellow squash, broccoli, cauliflower, bell peppers (red, yellow or green), onions, bok choy, celery, carrots, Portobello mushrooms, green beans, Brussels sprouts, etc.

- You can also steam green leafy veggies, such as Swiss chard, bok choy leaves, kale, collard greens, mustard greens, and beet greens. (You'll definitely want to steam the actual beets as well, but they're too messy to chop and store in advance.)

- For salads, choose lettuce, spinach, fresh herbs, cucumbers, tomatoes, radishes, etc.

- Store all produce in the refrigerator until ready to wash and chop if you're doing so the next day.

2 ~ wash & chop

- Fill sink about a third of the way up with water. Add produce wash as recommended on the bottle if using a commercial brand, or one of the homemade versions provided, to help dissolve any oil-based chemical sprays or waxes to which the produce may have been subjected.

- Place as many vegetables in water as possible and allow to soak for about 20 minutes. (You can also wash produce individually by spraying each piece, but this is more time consuming.) Scrub off any remaining dirt with a vegetable brush, rinse by running under clean , cool water and place washed produce in colander or clean dish rack.

- Towel dry vegetables before chopping to preserve freshness when stored. To dry leafy vegetables, use a salad spinner or lie flat in single layers on dish towels and blot carefully with another clean towel.

- Using a small serrated paring knife, cut off any bad spots.

- When chopping firmer vegetables to be used for steaming, roasting or grilling, chop vegetables that steam quickly, such as zucchini, into larger chunks, and vegetables that take longer to cook, such as broccoli or cauliflower, into small to medium-sized chunks.

- For salad and leafy greens, chop off the ends, separate, and chop the stems into bite-sized pieces. Tear the leaves with your fingers into manageable-sized pieces.

- Chop cucumbers, tomatoes, radishes and other veggies into bite-sized bits for salads and cold pasta dishes.

- It's also a good idea to chop some of the veggies, such as carrots and celery, into strips for dipping. And also to grate 3-4 cups of carrots (a food processor makes this task fast and easy!) to toss together with green salads or hide in pasta sauce.

3 ~ store

- Throw together all the firmer, chopped vegetables for steaming, grilling, or roasting in 1 or 2 *large* hard plastic or glass containers.

- Place salad and leafy greens in separate containers, preferably large zip-lock plastic bags or large hard plastic or glass containers.

- Place watery and other vegetables to be used in salads in separate containers, such as cucumbers, tomatoes, radishes, celery, etc. It's also a good idea to put chopped onions in a separate container as well, so as not to overpower the taste of the other vegetables.

- Produce will keep approximately 3-5 days chopped and stored in this manner depending on the type of produce, and how fresh it was when you bought it.

- You can double, and sometimes even triple, this storage time by vacuum sealing your chopped veggies. Learn how on the next page.

That's it. Follow these three easy steps—shop, wash & chop, and store—and you have a week's worth of fresh veggies (and more if you use a vacuum sealer) at your fingertips. You can throw raw veggies together for quick, colorful salads, and grab a handful or two of the mixed veggies as needed for cooking. Have these mixed veggies over rice or pasta with marinara sauce and a little grated, raw cheese or sprinkle of rice parmesan; add them to burritos, tacos, scrambled eggs, stir fry, lasagna or other casseroles, wraps or pita sandwiches.

You can now easily meet your daily quota by throwing veggies in everything you can think of! And at the end of the week, or when your once vibrant veggies first start to look a little sad, throw all the appropriate leftover veggies in a large pot with some broth and seasonings to make a delicious vegetable soup.

maximize time in the kitchen
While you're in the kitchen washing and chopping your vegetables is also the perfect time to put on a big pot of rice or other whole grains to cook. Make enough to last for a few days and store in convenient-sized containers, preferably vacuum sealing, if possible, for maximum storage time.

You can take these fast-food whole grains along for lunches, pull them out for quick dinners, or heat up with a few raisins and walnuts for hot cereal for breakfast in the morning. Another easy thing to do that will maximize this time in the kitchen, is to bake a few potatoes, yams, or sweet potatoes that can be reheated for lunches or dinners later.

I also know that it's popular with a lot of people to make food in advance and then freeze it. Unfortunately, I can't help much with this endeavor because I'm not a big fan of freezing. Whenever I do freeze foods, with the exception of lasagna, I end up throwing them out more than I eat them. If freezing homemade, healthier foods works for you however, by all means do it. Once again, it's a much better choice than a lot of others you could make.

The closer a food is to its whole, fresh, natural state, the higher its nutritional value.

Adopting this method of preparing vegetables and other foods in advance will increase your likelihood of eating more nutritious foods regularly at least ten-fold. Give it a try and see for yourself!

vegetable steamers

Steaming vegetables is a quick and easy way to get more of these nutrient-rich foods into your diet. The cheapest way to go is to purchase an accordion-type metal steamer insert that you can place in the bottom of pots you already have. Or you can invest in a large pot that comes with a steamer insert that sits on the top.

Fill the pot with 2-3 inches of water, place freshly-chopped vegetables in the steamer insert and cook to desired consistency. If you want, place denser vegetables that take longer to cook such as broccoli or cauliflower in the steamer first and cook for a couple minutes. Then throw in lighter veggies such as zucchini or yellow squash. Always cook leafy greens last by placing them on top and cooking for only the last minute or so or until they go limp.

To save even more time, try an automatic steamer or rice cooker such as the one pictured. Just fill it up, plug it in, set the timer and forget about it!

other tips & tidbits

- A vacuum sealer is a must-have for every healthy kitchen. It can save you so much time and money! Be sure to get one with a wide-mouth attachment to use with Mason jars. Also get a couple large hard plastic containers designed for your particular vacuum-sealer. Forget about the plastic rolls for sealing. They're expensive, hard to use and contribute to landfills.

- If you don't have a commercial salad spinner, place torn or chopped lettuce and other freshly washed green-leafy vegetables in an old pillow case—a clean one, of course!—hold the opening closed at the top, take outside and whirl around with your arm out stretched. Excess water will sprinkle out leaving you with dry leaves ready to use!

- Remember to eat a *variety* of vegetables. Try a new one every week to increase your choices. For recipe ideas, look for traditional dishes such as Indian, Asian and Middle Eastern, that frequently incorporate a medley of vegetables.

- It's easy to get 5-13 servings of fruits and vegetables a day into your diet—have 2 fresh fruits at breakfast and one for a mid-morning or mid-afternoon snack; have a big salad at lunch with 3-5 varieties of vegetables and a mixture of 3-5 steamed or grilled vegetables at dinner.

homemade produce wash

Add about 10 drops grapefruit seed extract to every 2 quarts pure water, when soaking produce in sink. Or, mix 10-20 drops with water in spray bottle to wash individual pieces of fresh produce.

OR...

Mix 2-3 ounces *Dr. Bronner's Natural All-Purpose Almond Soap* with 10 ounces purified water in spray bottle. Spritz on produce directly and rinse off, or add to water in sink for squeaky clean fruits and veggies.

No-Nonsense Nutrition

Article Series ~ By Kelly Hayford, CNC, Author *If It's Not Food, Don't Eat It!*

Eating Healthy When Eating Out

It's the frequency with which you eat out or attend food-related social gatherings that will determine how selective you need to be at any given outing. If you eat out virtually every day of the week for example, you're going to have to be as prudent as possible, as much as possible, when making food selections. If you only go out to eat once a month however, you can probably get away with eating whatever you like, if you are consistently eating well at home.

Since eating outside the home a few times a month or even a few times a week is the case for most people however, arming yourself with the following tips will help keep your intentions for good eating and good health on track.

social gatherings

For personal gatherings with family and friends, you can let your host or hostess know in advance that you're following a special diet. If they're close enough to you and it feels comfortable, you may like to share more details and even make special requests. You could also suggest bringing a dish to share that you know you'll be able to eat, so as not to have to trouble them with your particular needs. For potlucks, you can bring a dish or two of your liking as well, and just eat that when you get there without having to make any fanfare about it.

Another wise strategy to employ, whether you're planning to eat at a restaurant or attend a social gathering, is to eat before you go. This is especially helpful for situations in which you will have no control over what will be served, and know there will be little, if any, *real* food available.

If you eat before you go, you can just have a few nibbles when you get there without causing a lot of damage, or you can just socialize and not eat at all. Either way, plan in advance how you will deal with the situation and you'll greatly increase your chances of controlling it, rather than having it control you. Upcoming parties or special events are a great time to plan an indulgence you can look forward to, and keep yourself on track up until then. Just be sure the frequency with which you do so doesn't get out of hand.

eating at restaurants

When it comes to restaurant dining, you often have more control over your food choices. You can patronize those establishments that serve only whole, fresh, natural foods as much as possible, for example. Fortunately, at least in the more urban areas of the country, they seem to be popping up more and more. And, whether you're in a healthy restaurant or not, you can always choose what to order and how much to eat once it arrives.

Make the best menu choices possible and special requests if needed, to increase the nourishing nature of your meals. For instance, order salads with dressing on the side, steamed vegetables instead of French fries, or a cup of fresh fruit instead of a sugary muffin or toast.

Section 6, No. 4

Copyright 2008
Kelly Hayford

There isn't any condition in the body that can't be improved by improving your diet!

Unless you're dining at a restaurant that serves nouveau cuisine (you know, the ones that bring you a dab of food in the middle of a large plate with a drizzle across the top?), most restaurants today serve *way* more than what anyone should be eating in one sitting. Try these tips to help you avoid eating too much:

- *ask that the breadbasket or chips and salsa <u>not</u> be brought to the table as soon as you arrive*
- *or, take a reasonable portion out of the basket and place it on your serving plate to keep you from mindlessly eating straight from the basket until it's gone*
- *drink a cup of herbal tea or a large glass of water before your order arrives*
- *forgo appetizers before, and desserts after your meals*
- *order a healthy appetizer or a dish from the children's menu for your meal*
- *order pasta and a big salad and share it with your dining companion*
- *portion off your plate when it arrives*
- *ask that your plate be removed as soon as you're satisfied so you don't clean your own plate*
- *request that only half your order be brought to the table and have the rest doggie bagged for take home.*

Don't be afraid to assert yourself at restaurants. Remember that you're paying them to serve you. Be pleasant, however. That way you'll be more likely to get your requests fulfilled.

To avoid MSG, stay away from soups, dressings, and sauces. You can try asking the waiter, but because MSG can be hidden under many different names, even if they do check the label or ask the chef, they often still can't give you an accurate answer.

On more than one occasion at Asian restaurants, I have told the waitperson that I am highly allergic to MSG and they then directed me to dishes they swore did not contain it. A splitting migraine and a slew of other uncomfortable symptoms later, told me otherwise. After learning the hard way on too many occasions, I now only go to Asian restaurants that have a sign in their window that states unequivocally that they do not use MSG. Fortunately, there are a growing number of such health-minded restaurants around.

All of this talk about avoiding this, and switching this for that, reminds me of another very wise, all-important guideline for eating out: <u>on occasion</u>, *just go out and eat whatever you want, however much you want!* Seriously. You don't want to completely take the fun out of dining out. It's probably going to happen on occasion anyway, so you might as well give yourself permission rather than beating yourself up about it later. Please note, however, that I said <u>on occasion</u>, which should further be qualified as a *rare* occasion.

This unbridled occasion aside, it is best overall to limit the amount of time you eat out. The inclination to eat low-quality foods, and more of them, is just too great when you're eating out. Preparing foods at home, where you have total control over all ingredients, is always your best choice from a health and well-being standpoint, especially if you're trying to reverse a health condition.

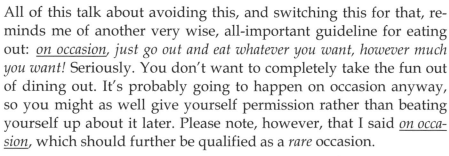

No-Nonsense Nutrition

Article Series ~ By Kelly Hayford, CNC, Author *If It's Not Food, Don't Eat It!*

Overcoming Obstacles to Eating for Health
Part 1 ~ Introduction & Obstacle #1: *It Takes Too Much Time!*

---

factoid: *How different our lives are when we really know what is deeply important to us, and keeping that picture in mind, we manage ourselves each day to be and to do what really matters most.*

— Stephen Covey

If you want to change the way you eat, you must change the way you think. That's what these next few articles are all about: exploring your current thoughts and beliefs about food and what you eat, so that you can begin to make informed, conscious choices that are in alignment with your values, rather than being a victim of subconscious beliefs you may not have even been aware existed.

Overcoming the mental obstacles to eating healthier is the single most important, yet most neglected or misunderstood aspect of making changes to your diet that people face today. For this reason, I have provided a generous amount of information here for you to get started. In addition, I highly recommend that you read *Section 2* of my book, *If It's Not Food, Don't Eat It!*, which will help you further.

the biggest obstacles
Over the last few years I have informally surveyed hundreds of people. Consistently they identify the following challenges as being the biggest obstacles when it comes to eating healthier:

1 ~ it takes too much time
    …to plan ahead and prepare healthy foods.

2 ~ it's too expensive
    …I can't afford to buy healthier foods.

3 ~ it's no fun
    …to eat healthy and be deprived of my favorite foods.

4 ~ it's too hard
    …to eat healthy foods when surrounded by a family, friends and a society that doesn't.

We will explore each in detail one by one. Doing so will help you begin to unravel your current thoughts and beliefs about food.

Like most people who do so, you will probably find that what you thought were big, bad insurmountable obstacles were nothing more than thoughts and beliefs you've held often unconsciously, for many years; unconscious thoughts that dictate your actions. Once you start re-evaluating and changing these thoughts and beliefs, these mental obstacles will begin to dissolve, and changes in the way you eat, will naturally and more easily occur as a result.

There isn't any condition in the body that can't be improved by improving your diet!

The best results are achieved by using the right amount of effort in the right place at the right time. And this right amount is usually less than we think we need.

— Michael Gelb

obstacle #1 ~ it takes too much time
...to plan ahead and prepare healthy foods.

This is sometimes a very real obstacle and there are a few other articles in this section with tips and information that can further help you address it. But it is just as often not the case as well.

In fact, making healthier choices can sometimes take even less time than some other less healthy choices. Having a piece of fruit or baby carrots or ready-to-eat salad for a snack, rather than toasting a bagel with cream cheese would be a good example. The same is often true when it comes to preparing meals. For example, it takes the same amount of time to steam some fresh vegetables as it does to pop a frozen entrée in the microwave and wait for it to cook. They both take an average of between 5-10 minutes.

Similarly, the challenge is often not about having the actual *time* involved that is the issue, but rather having the *energy* needed to prepare healthier foods. People, women with families especially, are frequently exhausted by the end of the day and just don't have the mental or physical energy to prepare meals from scratch.

This becomes a Catch-22 situation however, as the quick and convenient fake foods people resort to instead are so devoid of nutritional value that they *cause* a lack of energy and productivity. This can become a vicious cycle that can be challenging to break. However, with a little know-how it can be done more easily than you might think and the rewards you'll reap are well worth it.

expend initial energy to gain long-term energy
In a nutshell, the way to do it is to push through that initial transition period and expend the time and energy necessary to get yourself consistently eating energy boosting, health-promoting foods. If you can eat in accordance with the *Eating-for-Health Guidelines* as outlined, even if you have to *draaag* your behind into the kitchen to do it, you will eventually regain your energy. The length of

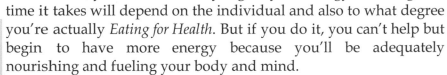

time it takes will depend on the individual and also to what degree you're actually *Eating for Health*. But if you do it, you can't help but begin to have more energy because you'll be adequately nourishing and fueling your body and mind.

Having more energy on a consistent basis translates into having more time, because you'll be more productive, need less sleep, take fewer naps, and generally feel better. So, when you think about it, eating poorly and the fatigue that inevitably goes along with it is what's really sucking up your time and energy!

time-saving strategies
To help with logistics, think about ways you can multi-task by combining food preparation and cooking with other activities.

For example, one client of mine listens to inspirational and educational tapes while she chops vegetables for the week. Another savors it as a kind of Zen-like meditation time, quieting her mind and reflecting on the events of the day. I like to plug in my headset to my cordless telephone and catch up with long distance friends and family members, or watch *Oprah* and the evening news programs. Enlisting the help of others can be another way of multi-tasking, especially with children.

People are frequently saying they'd like to spend more quality time with their children. Preparing food together can be just the opportunity. It's only been in recent decades in our modern Western society that we have adopted this idea that children's time should be spent playing or doing their homework rather than doing such things as helping in the kitchen. First of all, given the right attitude and approach, being involved in the preparation of food can be a source of great fun and fulfillment, play time if you will.

In addition, teaching children how to develop cooking and food preparation skills that will serve them for a lifetime is a worthy endeavor that in my opinion is equal to, and sometimes even more important than a lot of the homework they are required to do. One of the primary reasons many people, especially young adults, aren't eating as well as they could be today is because they never learned how to prepare and cook fresh foods. These are essential life skills for proper self care and the care of offspring.

Enrolling children and other household members to assist with food preparation and cooking is not only a great way to connect and spend quality time together, but will also cut down on the time you personally have to spend in the kitchen. Yes, it will require some initial time and patience for training, but the rewards are well worth the investment.

what do you *truly* value?

Another thing to consider when thinking about the time element involved with the preparation of healthy foods is how you spend your time in general. How you spend your time is a reflection of your values. Take a moment to think about where you might be wasting time that could be freed up in order to take better care of your nutritional needs—chit-chatting, watching T.V., reorganizing your sock drawer, complaining about how much you have to do and how little time you have to do it ?

Next ,think about prioritizing your time and making nourishing your body a top priority. I once worked with a woman who initially complained she had no time to cook for herself and her family because of her numerous outside obligations. She was on the board of two community organizations and belonged to at least another three. With all the meetings, fundraisers, and phone calls involved with these organizations, in addition to a successful full-time career, she had no time to take care of herself or her family. Or more accurately, she had plenty of time, but she chose to spend it in other ways.

As this woman's health started to deteriorate, she began to value taking care of herself more. Gradually she started to let go of her outside commitments, which certainly would not have been considered a waste of time by any means as they were all worthy causes. However, her ability to fulfill these obligations and maintain a balanced personal life as well was impossible.

The closer a food is to its whole, fresh, natural state, the higher its nutritional value.

It soon became clear to her that she was placing a higher value on others than she was on herself, and that she needed to make her own and her family's basic needs a top priority. With more time available, it then became a matter of retraining herself to create and integrate a routine of preparing and eating nutritious foods. Establishing routines is key.

establish routines

The more you start taking the time to eat healthier foods regularly, the less time consuming and easier it becomes. Think of those things that we are obligated to do as part of being in a human body that just become routine. Most people wouldn't think of going off to work without taking a shower, brushing their teeth, dressing, shaving, putting on makeup, etc. However, many of these same people complain that they don't have time to eat breakfast or pack a wholesome lunch.

Can you imagine walking into work naked and stubbly, with bad breath and body odor on a regular basis claiming you don't have time to get ready? It would never happen.

Sure there are days when you leave the stubble, lose the eyeliner, and throw on a baseball cap because you *really* didn't have the time or are taking a day off from the routine. But for the most part, you *make* the time to take care of these necessities for your benefit and the benefit of others. These hygeinic rituals have become ingrained routines that you automatically schedule in without giving them a second thought. It's just what you do. The same kind of automatic routines for healthy eating can be established as well.

Initially you'll have to go through a short transition period. However, once you have trained yourself to make the time and create routines around regularly eating healthier, you'll find that eventually it will become as routine as taking a shower and brushing your teeth every morning. Eventually you won't give it a second thought. It will just be what you do.

In fact, much like the days when you miss your morning shower, start feeling a little grungy and can't wait to take one, as you start to experience the many benefits of healthier eating—looking better, feeling better, having more energy, etc.—you'll find that you miss your healthier eating routines when you aren't able to follow them and can't wait to get back to them.

All in all, any time devoted to the preparation, cooking and enjoying of whole, fresh, natural foods is time well spent that serves you in all areas of your life. The same may be said of money spent on nutritious foods, which we will explore next.

quote:

We can no more afford to spend major time on minor things, then we can to spend minor time on major things!

— Jim Rohn

No-Nonsense Nutrition

Article Series ~ By Kelly Hayford, CNC, Author *If It's Not Food, Don't Eat It!*

Overcoming Obstacles to Eating for Health
Part 2: *It's Too Expensive!*

"Do you know what we call *Whole Foods Market* around our house?" a participant asked coyly when we got to the topic of food costs in an *Eating-for-Health* program, "We call it *Whole Paycheck!*"

Everyone laughed and nodded in agreement with this play on the name of the multi-chain natural foods store, including me. I knew exactly what she was driving at. She was essentially stating the second most frequently heard objection to *Eating for Health…*

obstacle #2 - it's too expensive
…I can't afford to buy healthier foods.

I have felt the bite of exorbitant grocery bills myself. However, over the years that I have been an avid consumer of health food, I have had many insights into this common complaint and now believe that all factors considered, it just isn't true.

If you think that you can't afford to eat healthier foods, I am here to tell you that you can't afford *not* to. There's nothing more expensive than poor health. And that is certainly what you will get from continually eating poor quality foods.

When you look at the bigger picture and consider the costs of doctor visits, drugs, diagnostic tests, surgeries and procedures, and time off work that can accrue due to poor health caused by a poor diet, you can begin to see how a little self-care via nutritious foods could easily pay off. If you were to compare these costs over time with the costs of healthier foods, you would find that prevention through proper nutrition is always cheaper.

quality of life
When thinking about food costs, in addition to the costs in terms of dollars, it's also wise to consider the costs in terms of quality of life. If you had extreme fatigue, headaches, sinus or stomach trouble on a regular basis, wouldn't you be willing to pay a few cents or a couple of extra dollars or so per day to get rid of these nagging symptoms?

That may be what you're doing already by purchasing over-the-counter or prescription drugs to treat these or similar *dis*-eases. Or some of you may be buying a double mocha latte every morning for the caffeine jolt you hope will get you jumpstarted. The problem is, these approaches merely mask the symptoms and ultimately contribute to the perpetuation of any current ailments, in addition to the possible development of new ones, because they tax the body and often have harmful side effects that go along with them.

Symptoms and *dis*-eases of the body and mind prevent you from living your life to the fullest. Not having enough energy or feeling well enough to play with your

Section 6, No. 6

Copyright 2008
Kelly Hayford

There isn't any condition in the body that can't be improved by improving your diet!

children, participate in recreational activities, or pursue your passions is a much higher price to pay than the little extra you might spend on better quality health-promoting foods.

what do you *truly* value?

Take a moment to reflect on where you currently put your dollars. What do you insist on spending a little extra to ensure better quality—clothes, furniture, jewelry, a luxury car? Are these conscious choices that reflect what you *truly* value in life, or have they developed over time and just become habit? How much are these choices influenced by society, family, friends, and colleagues?

In our modern society, although we claim otherwise, the care of our bodies and our health rank low when it comes to how we spend our money. Many people, for example, think nothing of spending exorbitant amounts of money every month on a new car and auto insurance payments, yet refuse to pay a few extra pennies or dollars for higher-quality foods.

Frequently, if you ask these same people what they value more, their family's health or their car, they will most assuredly tell you their family's health. But that's not what their spending habits say. More often than not, this is because they never really thought about it. It's just what people do these days. It's a consumer-driven cultural phenomenon. Similarly, most people are diligent about maintaining the health of their cars by taking them in for regular tune-ups, oil changes, etc., while completely neglecting their body's nutritional needs. As a society we currently spend more money on, and take better care of our cars than our bodies.

put your money where your mouth is!

Many people have the belief that eating health food costs more without ever having investigated the matter. Yes, most health-food brands of processed foods, such as salad dressings, pasta sauces, breads, etc., do cost a little more on average than the fake-food brands. But this is not what you want to be eating in great quantities anyway.

If you're eating whole, fresh, natural foods, such as produce, legumes and whole grains from the bulk bins, you'll be spending much less than what you would spend on processed foods of any kind and getting much greater nutritional value for your money. Organic produce used to be significantly more expensive across the board, but today it is often no more than, and occasionally even less than the non-organic produce. Check the prices and see for yourself.

Also consider that if you're truly *Eating for Health* you will not be spending money, or will be spending considerably less money, on expensive junk foods such as sugary cereals, soda, alcohol, snack foods, coffee, etc. You'll also be eating out less and dropping less money in vending machines—all of which add up to a smaller overall food bill. I could make a whole meal for two with leftovers on what some people spend every morning on their gourmet coffee and pastry to go!

When you take into account all the health benefits you derive and all the money you save on acute and chronic illness care now and in the future, all things considered *Eating for Health* is the best deal going. Put your money where your mouth is, literally! You'll be glad you did.

No-Nonsense Nutrition

Article Series ~ By Kelly Hayford, CNC, Author *If It's Not Food, Don't Eat It!*

Overcoming Obstacles to Eating for Health
Part 3: *It's NO Fun!*

Contrary to what many accustomed to the *Standard American Diet* believe, *Eating for Health* doesn't translate into pining for pizza and *Krispy Kremes* while you struggle to force down natural foods that taste like cardboard.

People who have integrated healthy eating as a lifestyle habit aren't walking around feeling deprived of foods they "can't" have and loathing those they do — at least not those that I know. Nor are they individuals who don't enjoy food, as I have heard some people suggest. People who regularly consume natural foods, health-food nuts if you will, enjoy food just as much as the next person. They have just come to enjoy and have fun with different foods. And that is the key.

The third most frequently voiced objection to *Eating for Health*...

obstacle #3 ~ it's no fun
...to eat healthy and be deprived of my favorite foods.

...is for the most part, a misconception that with a little understanding becomes much easier to uproot and toss aside so that it no longer stands in your way.

Yes, it's true that when endeavoring to eat differently as you first begin to let go of foods that are not serving you, *some* people will be mourning their losses. The most important thing to remember here is that this is a *temporary* situation.

Ask any health-food aficionado and they'll tell you that the long-term gains they have experienced were well worth any short-term fleeting challenges they had to go through to get them. Many will even tell you that they never experienced any feelings of loss or deprivation, that their body actually felt relieved as they embraced healthier foods and the nourishment they provided, leaving them feeling truly satiated, often for the first time in their lives.

health deprivation
It would be really wise to ponder this whole issue of perceived deprivation that you might encounter on the road to a better way of eating. Really get clear about what exactly you think you're going to be deprived of.

People are often attached to certain foods claiming they enjoy them immensely. They will indulge in these terrific tasting foods and feel magnificent for the few minutes it takes to chew and swallow them, then spend an entire day or night with unpleasant symptoms as a result — gas, bloating, stomach upset, sluggishness, headaches, etc. Doesn't sound very enjoyable to me.

And that's only their acute symptoms. They're frequently suffering from an array of chronic degenerative conditions as well, including excess weight, sinus problems, allergies, arthritis, diabetes, depression, heart disease, cancer and more

Section 6, No. 7

Copyright 2008
Kelly Hayford

There isn't any condition in the body that can't be improved by improving your diet!

One of the greatest human tragedies is when people continually indulge in shortsighted fleeting pleasures for fear of being deprived in the moment, only to find in the long run they have subjected themselves to the ultimate deprivation, the loss of their health. If you think healthy eating isn't any fun, ask yourself if being unhealthy is any fun? I can tell you from firsthand experience, it is not. If you're not *Eating for Health* you may already be experiencing health problems. If you're not, that is most assuredly the direction you're headed.

I want to clarify here that I think it's not only fun, but also healthy to indulge in what might otherwise be considered unhealthy foods just for the sheer pleasure of it. This, however, should be done only once in a while, such as once a week, once a month or once a quarter depending on the degree of decadence and your tolerance level.

are we having fun yet?

There are many people who express the sentiment, "Eat, drink and be merry, for tomorrow we die." Yes, of course we're all going to die sometime, but let's be optimistic and assume that you are going to live for at least a few more days, or months or years. Wouldn't you like to be *really* enjoying each of the days before that time and spend them doing the things you love to do?

Often the people I hear express that they're "going to eat what they want and enjoy themselves," are people that aren't really enjoying themselves at all. They're sick and fat and tired and complaining about all their aches and pains and doctor bills and not having the energy to do anything.

When people are on their deathbeds they most frequently express regret for the things they never did in life. I believe many people, at least in our modern world, never do many of the things they'd love to do in life because they're too sick, tired or depressed to get out there and do them! Do you seriously think you're going to be on your deathbed regretting that you didn't eat more pizza or ice cream or chocolate cake? For many it's quite the opposite.

I'll never forget my mother saying to me during her first unexpected stay in the hospital, "I wish I had taken better care of myself. I probably wouldn't be in here right now." She then vowed that given a second chance she would start eating better once she was discharged and asked me for help. Unfortunately, she never got that second chance. This turned out to be the first in a succession of lengthy hospital stays she had to endure until she died almost a year later. In the end, she felt that her neglectful habits had deprived her of precious months, possibly years of her life.

This was not fun for her. She was only 63. She had a new grandbaby, friends and family that loved her, and an award-winning career as an artist. She wasn't ready to go. She knew she could have eaten better and exercised, and she regretted not having done so when she'd had the opportunity.

If you're reading this article you still have the opportunity. Seize this opportunity, do it for yourself and your loved ones. *Eating for Health* is much more fun than depriving yourself of the quality and possibly the quantity of life to which you're entitled. Seize the day—you won't regret it!

factoid : *Americans lose on average 15 years of life from chronic diseases — valuable time with family or friends gone forever. Chronic disease accounts for 70% of all deaths in the United States.*

— Centers for Disease Control and Prevention

No-Nonsense Nutrition

Article Series ~ By Kelly Hayford, CNC, Author *If It's Not Food, Don't Eat It!*

Overcoming Obstacles to Eating for Health
Part 4: *It's Too Hard!*

The fourth most frequently voiced objection to *Eating for Health* on a regular basis is admittedly the most legitimate and challenging...

obstacle #4 - it's too hard
...to eat healthy foods when surrounded by a family, friends and a society that doesn't.

Yes, it can be very hard to adopt and maintain a healthier eating lifestyle when surrounded by family members and coworkers who don't, not to mention having to resist the vending machine down the hall at work, the banquet table covered with unhealthy food at every social gathering, and the drive-thru window of fast-food emporiums that beckon to you from every main street corner.

It can be tremendously challenging. There's no doubt about it. Use what you're learning here and persevere. It will get easier and easier, I promise. Following are a few suggestions that can be helpful.

the impact of cultural influences
We as a society are in the midst of what could be described as a manic episode when it comes to our relationship with our bodies and our diets. You must understand how this is affecting you at a personal level in order to make it easier to get out from under it.

Food manufacturers spend over $34 billion a year on making sure you're aware of their nutritionally-bankrupt food products. In one year alone, McDonald's spends $1 billion in advertising, in stark contrast to the governments *5-A-Day Program*, which spent a mere $2 million in its peak year. To fathom the vast difference, ponder the following:

- *1 million seconds = 10.4 days*
- *1 billion seconds = 32 years*

When you consider the magnitude with which we are being deluged with multi-media advertising campaigns designed by leading psychologists to infiltrate our minds and manipulate our behavior, you can't help but conclude that we are being subjected to a kind of bad-food brainwashing. And, as the dramatic changes in our eating habits show, it's working.

Many people's way of thinking has been radically altered by this insidious assault on their psyches, often to the point of overriding their common sense when it comes to making food choices. For example, I have encountered many people who are afraid to eat eggs, a whole, fresh, natural food that has helped sustain generations, but don't think twice about slurping down one or more sodas per day, loaded with sugar, caffeine, and a host of other *dis*-ease-causing chemical additives. This defies logic, and is a prime example of how extremely imbalanced our popular food culture has become.

Because it has become so skewed, even a small deviation in the direction towards health-producing foods is still frequently a long, long way from what is natural or healthful. It may now be *normal* in our modern Western society to eat 90% processed foods, but it's still completely un-*natural*. Even eating natural-brand foods is completely unnatural, as they are still *processed* foods.

Another factor contributing to our bad-food mania is the fact that processed food has become very cheap, very abundant, and very available. In the last two decades the amount of food produced in the U.S. has increased 500 calories per person per day; the price of food in both stores and restaurants has fallen; and there are now an estimated 320,000 different processed, packaged foods. This dramatically influences what we eat, when and how much.

Never before in history have we had so many poor food choices so readily obtainable and so affordable. People used to be limited to the amount of food their livestock could produce and their fruit tree could bear, which was frequently not enough. Today we are inundated with an inordinate amount of low-quality, low-cost, seductive food. We can't get away from it!

To compound the problem, there's an equally excessive amount of polarized and conflicting nutritional information we receive, both in general and with regard to specific foods. Despite this flood of what is often pseudo- or incomplete scientific information, our diets and state of health isn't getting better, it's getting worse. Clearly, this route is not the answer.

The real road to attaining a sustainable diet and resultant better state of health lies in the nutritional knowledge and understanding that has stood the test of time. In order to do so, remember that we are in a cultural era of *extreme* poor eating and shed unwanted social conditioning as much as possible.

the art of selective perception
One thing that can be worthwhile in undoing some of this bad-food brainwashing is developing the art of selective perception. To give you an idea of what I mean, a couple of years ago a woman was giving me directions to a function. She told me to turn left at the Burger King on the corner, approximately a mile from my house. Although I had lived in the neighborhood for several years and had driven by there hundreds of times, I had no idea where the Burger King was. When I told her so, she laughed in dismay and then remembered that I was a health-food nut.

"Wow, you mean you really don't even notice places like Burger King?" she exclaimed. "I wish I could do that, I'd probably be able to lose that extra 20 pounds!"

I honestly don't notice fast-food places anymore. They're like noise on the side of the road to me. In the past I could have told you where every fast-food restaurant was within a 20 mile radius, along with every item on their menu and their prices. Today I couldn't tell you the fast-food joints that I drive by every day, but I could tell you where every natural foods store and restaurant is this side of the Mississippi (a slight exaggeration, but close!).

This selective perception developed naturally over the course of time, as it will for you the more you start to eat better. To help accelerate the process, when you see your favorite fast-food or other not-such-a-healthy-choice restaurant and you get a pitter patter of excitement—STOP! and see how fast you can think of other choices that would serve you better health-wise. For example, going to the café down the street that serves fresh salads, or a nearby grocery store where you could pick up a roast chicken or an additive-free, natural brand frozen entrée. You may still give in and go for the triple-decker cheeseburger with everything and a jumbo milk shake, but at least you made a *conscious* choice.

Similarly, you can also begin to make it a point to set your radar for natural foods stores and restaurants. Doing so helps you to expand your thoughts about what is available to you. This is really important in this day and age, as most people's brains tend to be on automatic pilot, set in the direction of our degenerate popular food culture, which frequently prevents them from even recognizing other possibilities.

STOP!—and make the association

Another thing that can make it easier to psyche yourself up for healthier eating is to begin to make the conscious association between how you feel and the foods you eat. Whenever you find yourself thinking healthy eating is too hard--STOP! and ask yourself, is it any easier to have a headache, stomach ache, arthritis, heart attack, sinus problems or any other *dis*-eases you are currently experiencing, or could potentially experience as a result of eating this food?

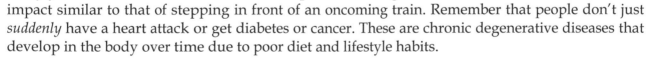

If you step out in front of an oncoming train going 100 miles an hour, the consequences you face are clear and immediate. When it comes to the food you eat however, the consequences of your choices are often neither clear nor immediate. As a result, you often don't make the association between the two. The more that you can train yourself to make a direct correlation between symptoms or *dis*-eases and the foods you're eating, the easier it becomes to make better food choices.

Continuously making poor food choices over the course of many years can result in *dis*-eases that are capable of having an impact similar to that of stepping in front of an oncoming train. Remember that people don't just *suddenly* have a heart attack or get diabetes or cancer. These are chronic degenerative diseases that develop in the body over time due to poor diet and lifestyle habits.

The same is true of non-life threatening, albeit equally annoying, conditions such as arthritis, sinus problems, depression and the like. The more that you can keep this in mind and remember it when faced with having to choose between a healthy and not-so-healthy food choice, the easier it will become to make the choice that is best for you.

practice, practice, practice

Practicing any new skill or behavior regularly is what leads to mastery. Because it is a lifelong process, not an event, this is especially true when it comes to healthy eating. The key to success is consistent action over time. So, if you fall off the proverbial horse, keep getting back on. Whether you're learning to ride a horse or a bike, or are trying to quit smoking, exercise regularly or eat healthy consistently, if you want to conquer the beast you've got to keep trying and practicing until you get it right.

The closer a food is to its whole, fresh, natural state, the higher its nutritional value.

Studies show that it takes 6-7 tries on average before a person is able to quit smoking for good. I believe the same is true for healthy eating. So, if you've tried to adopt and maintain a healthier eating lifestyle a few times already and have failed, that's the good news. It means you're almost there! So whatever you do, don't give up now.

Just think if you had given up the first couple of times you toppled over when first learning to ride a bike because it was too hard. You never would have learned how. Even though it was challenging to start, didn't it get easier each time you fell off and got back on? Eventually it wasn't hard at all and you just cruised right along. That's how *Eating for Health* will become for you if you just keep at it.

the pain of withdrawal is temporary

Speaking of quitting smoking, there are a lot of similarities between this health-robbing habit and poor eating. Another similarity that is important for you to be aware or reminded of is the withdrawal phase that often comes along with both. Everyone knows that when trying to quit smoking, many people suffer from acute withdrawal symptoms such as headaches, fatigue, nervousness, irritability and cravings for nicotine.

What many people don't know however, is that when transitioning to a more nutritious diet and letting go of certain foods, you may experience similar withdrawal symptoms as the body seeks to rebalance its internal environment. This is especially true if you consume a lot of processed pseudofoods and the extreme stimulating foods such as coffee and sugar. It's critical that you understand this and expect it if you decide to go cold turkey on certain foods so that you can arrange your schedule and otherwise prepare yourself.

Don't let the thought of withdrawal scare you off though. You'll be so much better off once you get to the other side. Isn't a smoker better off having gone through an acute withdrawal period in order to rid himself of this life extinguishing habit than to have kept smoking?

the other-human interaction factor

All well and fine, you say, if I were on my own. However, most people are immersed in a community that includes immediate and extended family members, friends, colleagues, co-workers, and various other human beings. Co-habitation and social get-togethers with these numerous other humans almost always involves food, which can indeed be a problem.

Because it can pose challenges of such great magnitude, there's an entire chapter devoted to dealing with this other-human interaction factor in my book, *If It's Not Food, Don't Eat It!* If this is a big issue for you I highly recommend that you read it for more help. In a nutshell, it's important that you associate with people who are supportive of your efforts to adopt a healthier eating lifestyle and avoid those who are not. This is especially important in the beginning stages of your transition.

You obviously can't avoid family members and those that are closest to you, however. When it comes to them it is best to focus on yourself and lead by example. Having a heart-to-heart talk with them as outlined next, can also be tremendously helpful.

No-Nonsense Nutrition

Article Series ~ By Kelly Hayford, CNC, Author *If It's Not Food, Don't Eat It!*

Section 6, No. 9

Copyright 2008
Kelly Hayford

"The Talk" for Gaining Support
Tips for a Heart-to-Heart with Loved Ones

quote: *The educating of one's environment is a constant, natural and eventually effortless process, but it may take a while to reeducate the folks and things in your life on how you now want them to be or provide for you.*

And it will take time for you to access the exact language you need to say what you want to say and to get what you need without having to strain your self or the other person.

— Thomas Leonard

Because those closest to you are the ones who have the biggest effect on you and are the most affected *by* you and your decision to make new dietary choices, it is wise to take the time and forethought to engage in a good old-fashioned heart-to-heart with them about what is going on for you.

The most obvious people you would want to have this talk with would be immediate family members, significant others and anyone else who lives with you. You may also want to have a modified version of this talk with close friends or co-workers that you dine with regularly (or drink beer with, as the case may be). Either way, there are certain guidelines that are wise to follow and specific points you'll want to make in order to get the most out of this conversation.

Our relationships with others are very individualized, so you'll want to spend some time thinking about what's most appropriate for you and each person you'll be talking to. Following is a list of top ten suggestions that can help:

1 ~ set the time and space for the talk
…to demonstrate its importance and ensure you have your listener's undivided attention.

During the commercial break of your spouse's favorite T.V. program or at the breakfast table when the kids are running late for school are obviously not the best time or setting to have your heart-to-heart talk with them. You'll either want to set an official date or plan it for when you know you will have uninterrupted time, such as a lengthy car drive. Also be sure to allow enough time to have a leisurely conversation. So often in our high-paced contemporary lives we tell each other things in passing, only to have them forgotten because our attention was somewhere else.

By setting a special time and date to have a talk, you're demonstrating the importance of what you have to say and will ensure that you have your listener's full attention. You may want to have some healthy snacks for the person you'll be talking with to give them a little taste of what you're learning—which would be helpful in the public relations department as well ;-)

2 ~ include all members of the family
...when you have this talk, even the little ones.

You may want to speak with them separately, but be sure you talk to all members of the family no matter what their age, even infants and toddlers. Little ones understand more than we give them credit for and they appreciate being included. Even though they may not understand your every word, they hear and respond when you speak from your heart. They understand your general intentions and are happy to have been included in whatever is going on.

3 ~ focus on yourself
...use sentences that begin with "I" and speak from your heart.

When we start to make personal changes, especially changes important enough to require help, it can sometimes make those close to us feel a little uncomfortable. Keeping the focus on yourself and using statements beginning with "I" (i.e., I would like some help..., etc.), is not only less threatening, but also helps others to more clearly understand what you are saying, both of which will greatly increase the odds that you will be heard and receive a favorable response. Another effective approach is to put yourself in the other person's shoes and think about how you would want to be addressed and what would help you to be more receptive.

4 ~ tell them what you're doing and why
...with regard to your decision to make changes in your diet and develop a healthier eating lifestyle.

Tell them that you're learning lots of new and interesting things about food and healthier eating that you're trying to integrate in your own life. Share with them specific reasons you want to do this (i.e., lose weight, relieve digestive disturbances, etc.). Also, be sure to include any reasons that may relate to them in particular (i.e., you want to increase your energy so that you can play baseball with them, make mad passionate love to them, etc.). They will be very happy to hear these reasons and will be more likely to lend support. Be honest however; people can see right through insincerity and you don't want to say anything that could come back to haunt you.

5 ~ invite them to join you
...but let them know that you honor, accept and respect them if they don't.

This fifth suggestion primarily applies to other adults and older teens in your life who are in a position to make decisions for themselves. This is a great opportunity to let them know that because you love and care about them you would love for them to start eating healthier too. Remember to keep using those "I" statements. For example, "I would love for you to join me and start eating healthier, too," versus "*You need* to start eating healthier too."

These are two very different approaches and will elicit very different responses. Nobody likes to be told what to do. With younger children in your care however, you are in a position to be telling them what to do until they are old enough to make decisions for themselves. This would be a good time to let them know that because it is your responsibility to care for and nourish them, you will be helping them to discover new healthier foods that they will enjoy as well.

6 ~ tell them what to expect
...from you as you are making the transition.

Sometimes when people start making changes to their diet, especially if they're getting off any extreme addictive foods such as sugar or caffeine, they will feel tired, cranky, headachy or otherwise

Section 6, No. 9 ~ "The Talk" for Gaining Support continued...

out of sorts temporarily as their bodies adjust. This same kind of withdrawal experience can happen when eliminating some other foods as well, especially any of the common food allergens such as wheat, dairy or soy. This is something you not only want to be aware of and prepare for yourself, but this is also information you'll want to share with those closest to you who may be affected by any changes in your mood or behavior.

Plan as little as possible for the first critical days in which you're weaning yourself off these foods, including letting others know how you might be feeling and asking them to give you some space to go through it. Also, let them know that there will be certain things you will no longer want or be willing to do that you may have done together in the past, such as going to certain restaurants or indulging in certain treats. Giving them a heads up now will help avert problems down the road.

7 ~ make specific requests
...as to how they can show their support and help you.

Tell them you would really appreciate their support and make very specific requests as to how they can provide it. You will want to think about this before you sit down to talk so you can make the most of this opportunity to ask for help. Set your listener and yourself up for success by making no more than 1-3 clear, simple requests that can easily be accomplished. For example, "Please don't entice me to go to Dairy Queen and have a double fudge banana split," "Walk the dog after school so I have more time to prepare a nutritious meal," "Give me a dozen roses instead of a box of chocolates for Valentine's Day," or whatever is appropriate for you. You can always make future requests and take things to the next level once the first ones have been integrated, but keep it very simple and doable to start.

8 ~ do not advise them
...about their eating habits at this time, this talk is about you.

Don't use this time to nag them about what you think they "should" or "shouldn't" or "need" to be doing. Remember this talk is about *you* and your requests for support. Keep these issues completely separate or you will, no doubt, sabotage your efforts on both fronts.

9 ~ be brief and to the point
...to make it easier for them to hear what you're saying and grant your requests.

Think in advance about what you would like to say. You may even like to jot down a few notes if you need to, so that when it comes time for the talk, you can be as brief and to the point as possible. Don't ramble on and on, or get off track on other topics, or you run the risk of losing your listener's attention and possibly their support. The more precise and poignant you can be, the better chance of being heard and receiving a favorable response.

10 ~ politely remind and repeat
...them of points you have made in your talk in the days to come until new routines are established.

Just because you sat down and had this talk doesn't mean that your listeners are going to remember everything you said, and immediately begin fulfilling all your requests. Remember that this issue is important to *you*, not them. Don't get mad when they forget things you have told them. *Expect* that they will forget and that you will have to politely remind them. It will take a little time

The closer a food is to its whole, fresh, natural state, the higher its nutritional value.

and repetition before they are able to develop new patterns of behavior. Repeat commitments or requests you have made nicely and often, until they become integrated into your collective life-style.

stretch your comfort zone

These top ten suggestions will be a tremendous help to you when talking to your dear ones about your intentions to create a healthier eating lifestyle for yourself and garner their help as well. Do take the time to have this talk with your loved ones even if it feels a little out of your comfort zone. It will pay off in the long run and help you to move in the direction you want to go.

As for other people in your life who don't fall into this close-quarters category such as friends or extended family members, but who may still be affected by the changes you're making, it's wise to have a modified version of this heart-to-heart talk as mentioned, or address the topic as it comes up. Whatever fits best for that particular relationship.

Regarding more casual relationships such as co-workers or fellow members of the P.T.A., unless there's a specific reason to do so, there's no need to broadcast the fact that you're undergoing a nutritional transformation. Especially in the beginning, when you haven't quite rooted yourself in this transformation, it's often smart to keep this matter private. Otherwise, you run the risk of opening yourself up to criticism, teasing and even heated discussions, all of which are better avoided.

Of course, whether you say anything or not, people will begin to notice your absence from the buffet table you used to loiter around, or your unwillingness to pick up that box of Krispie Kremes on the way into work, for example. In those instances, if someone inquires, unless you're certain they will be supportive, it's best to keep your response brief and go with a simple one-liner or two. "Double fried chicken wings just don't agree with me anymore," "I'm allergic to dairy products," "Yep, I'm cutting down on the sweets," are all good responses that require no further explanation.

When met with someone you are certain will *not* be supportive, and who may also be predisposed to teasing or arguing (we all know one or more of these type people), it's best to keep quiet and smile, or give a little giggle to any insulting or aggressive comments and make a gracious exit if possible. No use subjecting yourself to such treatment when you're trying to do something nurturing for yourself.

Some people can get really funny about food and beverages. Even though you may be talking about what *you* are doing, if it isn't in agreement with what *they're* doing or pushes their guilt buttons about what they think inside they *should* be doing, some people can get testy and take it out on you. As much as possible, especially in the early stages of making changes in your diet and lifestyle, it's best to associate with those who are supportive of your efforts and avoid those who are not.

quote: *Who are you around, what have they got you thinking, what have they got you saying, what have they got you doing, where do they have you going?*

— Jim Rohn

You are what you eat and you are also what you don't eat—eat well, be well.

No-Nonsense Nutrition

Article Series ~ By Kelly Hayford, CNC, Author *If It's Not Food, Don't Eat It!*

Try It, You'll Like t!
Training Your Taste Buds to Enjoy *Real* Food

It's imperative to understand that taste is *acquired* and it can be *un*-acquired as well. I guarantee that given the right amount of time, which will be different for everyone, once you start eating natural foods regularly your taste buds will acclimate and you won't feel deprived. On the contrary, you'll discover new foods you'll come to love even more and you'll feel good about eating them on all levels. Trust me on this one. I've seen it happen numerous times.

People who give up poor-quality, albeit tasty foods frequently come back and tell me I was right about this. They *don't* feel deprived or miss those things they used to die for (literally!). In fact, most don't even have a taste for them anymore and many have actually developed a *dis*taste for foods they used to love. On average it takes about 8 weeks to change your palate—but for many it can happen sooner.

give yourself a *real* treat

Treats are definitely one of the things people are afraid they will miss if they start eating better. First of all, this is not what *Eating for Health* advocates doing. Instead, see what you can do about progressively upgrading the *quality* of your treats, and also intentionally scheduling them in and having them only once in a while as a planned indulgence, if you will.

Secondly, think for a moment of the most scrumptious, no holds barred treat you can think of. How often do you have it? How often do you treat yourself to this treat? Let's just say it's a double hot-fudge sundae with a boatload of delectable toppings. Now, think about having this sugary, crunchy, syrupy delight every day, three times a day. Does it still seem like a treat? Would you even want to do this? When you think of having it this often it starts to lose its appeal, doesn't it?

When you allow yourself to have something every day or on a very regular basis, you are effectively diminishing its special treat status. A real treat is something that is not only a special delight, as my dictionary says, but there is also a frequency of indulgence factor involved here as well. If, for example, you have ice cream and cookies before you go to bed every night, going out for ice cream and cookies is no longer a special treat because you do it every night. You are in essence depriving yourself of treats.

try it, you'll like it!

"I hear everything you're saying, but my problem is I can't stand the taste of vegetables," a young woman once confided to me. This is a common complaint I have heard from others as well. In the infamous style of tell-it-like-it-is Dr. Phil McGraw, my response to this complaint in short, is—get over it!

Chances are, there are several things you didn't like at first, but later learned to love. Coffee and alcoholic beverages are a good example. Unless you were one of those rather odd children who liked to sip from Uncle Fred's beer can at family picnics, or grandma's coffee mug at the kitchen table, you probably wrinkled up your face with disgust the first time you tasted these pungent adult beverages. But most of you kept on drinking them anyway when you came of age, because you wanted the 'buzz' and the 'cool' status that came along with them. You essentially *forced* yourself to learn to like these drinks, to the extent that many of you actually came to love them.

It's interesting to ponder that as a society we think nothing of training ourselves to acquire tastes for things that are unhealthy, such as coffee and alcohol, yet balk at the notion of training ourselves to acquire tastes for things that are good for us, such as broccoli and Brussels sprouts. Similarly, we don't think twice about eating fake foods saturated with harmful amounts of fat, sodium, sugar and toxic chemical additives.

We have become very complacent about what we put in our mouths. Quite often, people don't have a clue what's in the food they're eating and they don't care either. As long as it tastes good and everyone else is eating it, it's O.K. Would you knowingly eat rat poison just because it tasted good and was the popular thing to do? Of course not. Yet, that's essentially what we've been conditioned to do, albeit on a slightly lesser, but nonetheless damaging scale. The primary criterion for making food choices should be the quality of the food and its benefits to the body, with taste as the secondary factor. You can have both, to be sure. But to put your taste buds and social acceptance before your health and well-being is a recipe for disaster.

burned out buds

If you currently find vegetables and other healthy foods distasteful, chances are your taste buds are accustomed to the unnatural faire of the *Standard American Diet*. Because of their extreme nature, these highly-refined foods with their artificial flavorings and excessive amounts of sugar, refined salt and bad fats, literally burn out your taste buds. If this is the case, and it is for most people, don't despair. While you may never develop a taste for Brussels sprouts (I certainly haven't!), you *can* develop tastes for healthier foods and believe it or not, actually come to prefer them.

Know that it *can* be done and that with time you will get an even better 'buzz' from eating natural, nutrient-rich foods; a constant buzz of strength, energy, emotional balance, and overall health and well-being. All this, instead of the highs and lows—which eventually turn into primarily lows— that you get from eating unnatural, nutrient-poor foods, including overly stimulating substances such as caffeine, alcohol, refined salt and sugar.

tricks of the trade

A tried and true method of helping to train your taste buds is to have a dish or food item on 5 different occasions and have 5 bites each time you have it. This frequently helps people develop tastes for new, healthier foods because taste is a lot about familiarity. Also try having foods prepared in different ways. You may find that you don't like broccoli raw, but it tastes O.K. steamed or with a certain kind of sauce, for example. Of course there will be things you flat-out don't like, but give these little tricks a try for the things that at least have a chance. Who knows, the things you try may one day become some of your favorites!

No-Nonsense Nutrition

Article Series ~ By Kelly Hayford, CNC, Author *If It's Not Food, Don't Eat It!*

Helping Children Eat Healthier

factoid: *Researchers say that for the first time in a century, today's children can look forward to a shorter life expectancy than their parents.*

— Texas Children's Hospital Study

In recent decades the food industry has aimed their heaviest marketing artillery at the most impressionable and vulnerable segment of our society, with the intention of creating lifelong consumers of their fake-food products. It's now evident that they didn't just hit their target, they got a bull's eye. Our children have been hit and they've been hit hard. The health statistics that are just now starting to emerge as a result of this hit are the scariest of all.

For the first time in history, conditions that were previously associated with aging are now showing up in children at younger and younger ages. *Dis*-eases such as Type 2 diabetes, high cholesterol, high blood pressure, and even heart attacks, have now reached unprecedented and rapidly increasing numbers among our youth.

We have a moral obligation as the stewards of this next generation to do everything in our power to turn this trend around and give our children every opportunity to live normal, healthy lives. We're not only robbing them of their childhoods, but the quality of their adulthoods, and possibly their very lives as well.

Despite the troubling predictions and burgeoning health crisis that is emerging, an abundant supply of soda, junk food and pseudofood continues to flow into the mouths of our youngsters. One of the most alarming dispensaries of these anti-nutrients is in the very place children should be the safest from manipulative marketing maneuvers—our public schools.

roar, mama roar!

We don't allow tobacco companies to put their vending machines at the end of school hallways. In fact, even advertising for tobacco products is banned within a certain radius of school grounds. As a society, we have become adamant about sending out a clear message to our youth that smoking cigarettes is hazardous to their health. Why then do we allow vending machines in school hallways, *serve* disease-causing junk food in school cafeterias, and allow fast-food franchises to place the majority of their restaurants in close proximity to schools?

Statistically speaking, these health-robbing foods cause far greater harm than tobacco. It's unconscionable to be taking advantage of this most precious and vulnerable segment of our society in this way. We should be sending out a clear message to our youth that junk food is hazardous to their health as well.

The good news is, you have complete control over what travels across the threshold of your house and makes its way into your cupboards. This is also where you have the most influence. The more you clean up your own diet and restore your own health and energy, the more you will be an energetic dynamo and role model for helping your children. But you don't have to wait. Jump on the bandwagon now and get it rolling!

same guidelines apply

Once adults make the leap onto the healthy-eating-for-children bandwagon, the first thing they want to know is what to feed the young 'uns. Guess what? It's simple. The same *Eating-for-Health Guidelines* apply.

When considering the guidelines as they apply to children, you'll want to magnify their importance ten-fold. Children's smaller, still developing bodies are much more sensitive to low-quality anti-nutrient foods and the many noxious substances they contain, such as MSG, food colorings, preservatives, etc. They are also hypersensitive to stimulants such as sugar and caffeine. Unfortunately, the pseudofoods made especially for the younger age bracket are loaded with all of the above.

So many children's delicate bodies and brains aren't able to function properly because they're not getting the nutrients they need. At the same time they are taking in anti-nutrients and stimulants that further interfere with their ability to function normally. There are millions of children today thought to have a host of conditions who are in fact merely lacking proper nutrition.

Take any child off processed, packaged pseudofoods, sugar, caffeine and any common food allergens to which they may be sensitive (i.e., follow the *Eating-for-Health Guidelines*), and you will see a significant improvement in their behavior and physical well-being, no matter what conditions they currently may or may not have. Feed them lots of whole, fresh, natural foods and be sure they're getting an adequate amount of essential fatty acids and green foods (the two things most missing from the *Standard American Diet)* and the changes you'll see take place will astound you.

make nutrition a priority

Unless your child is having an acute situation that demands immediate intervention please, please do not subject your children to dangerous, traumatic surgeries, procedures, and toxic drugs until you have explored safe, natural approaches that emphasize nutritional factors.

There are thousands of surgeries performed every year on children who have had recurrent ear infections, for example; surgeries that could have been prevented by identifying and eliminating offending foods from the child's diet. As previously mentioned, doctors are not always familiar with, nor have the appropriate diagnostic tools for this task. Either do some research and experi-

menting on your own or work with a holistic practitioner who is knowledgeable about food allergies and intolerances that can help you.

Whether your child is presently experiencing any health challenges or not, you'll still want to place a high priority on the foods they eat. The younger children are when they begin to eat harmful foods and miss out on the nourishing foods their body needs, the more likely they are to develop chronic *dis*-ease in the future and at a younger age, whether they currently have symptoms or not. Children's bodies respond quickly to changes in diet one way or the other. Feed them well and they'll thrive. Feed them foolishly and they'll nose dive.

Section 6, No. 11 ~ Helping Children Eat Healthier continued...

I have a friend who runs a day care facility with a 'nothing-sweeter-than-fruit allowed' policy. She feeds the children whole, fresh, natural foods and no sweets other than fresh fruit. This is by far the most focused, orderly, relaxed, cooperative group of small children I have ever seen. There are very few squabbles and also very few absences due to illness. These children thrive. They don't feel as though they're missing out on soda or junk food. Some of them aren't even yet aware that it exists. Those who are, are being taught a valuable lesson. They are being taught to keep junk food and processed pseudofood to a minimum, and to have them only on rare, social occasions rather than as daily faire.

By now I hope you are convinced that helping your children to eat well is essential, and based on the universal *Eating-for-Health Guidelines*, you should have a pretty good idea of *what* to feed them. But I know what many of you are probably thinking now—actually getting them to eat better is another story.

practical strategies

The best advice for helping children establish well balanced eating habits is to start from the beginning by feeding them primarily whole, fresh, natural foods (80-100%), minimal amounts of naturally processed foods (0-20%), and absolutely no junk foods or pseudofood brands. Keeping kids away from extreme tasting junk and pseudofood is the only sure way to prevent them from developing a taste for it. If it's too late for that, systematically transition them off the undesirable foods and re-educate their wayward palates.

This is not as difficult as people sometimes think. I have seen scores of parents transform their children's dietary habits with little to no trouble. And yes, all of them thought "not my kids!" at first, just as many of you may be thinking now. Although some will fight and kick and scream initially, children learn, make changes, and adapt more easily than adults. Once made aware of, and taken off the foods that are overriding their natural sensibilities, kids are often surprisingly more attuned to their instinctual desire for initiating and maintaining a nutritious diet.

Don't rob children of the opportunity to establish good eating habits that will serve them for a lifetime. Developing self-care skills is a critical and sorely neglected part of their education. You must rise to the occasion and make your responsibility bigger than your excuses. Make use of all the information in this book, which can easily be applied to children and the quick tips on the next page.

You must place the same importance on good nutrition in your household as you do on wearing seat belts in your car. Seventy percent of deaths in America are due to chronic degenerative disease and the average American loses 15 years of their life to these largely preventable *dis*-eases. So, statistically speaking allowing children to indulge in poor eating habits is even *more* dangerous than driving without their seat belts on. Make your words and actions convey the danger of poor nutrition and the value of good nutrition to your children .

factoid: *At Texas Children's Hospital, the percentage of children and adolescents diagnosed with type 2 diabetes increased from less than 1% twenty years ago to 27% in 2002.*

The closer a food is to its whole, fresh, natural state, the higher its nutritional value.

You are what you eat and you are also what you don't eat—eat well, be well.

factoid: *A study of children ages six through eight found that 70% believed that fast foods were healthier than food from the home.*

— Dr. Kelly Brownell, *Food Fight*

quick tips for helping kids eat better

1 ~ Appeal to their interests by making them aware of the many benefits they will derive from eating healthy (i.e. every child wants to be strong, healthy, fast, smart, etc.).

2 ~ Educate them about what are wise food choices and how to make them, and avoid making sweeping statements such as "that food is bad for you", etc.

3 ~ Involve them with food preparation as much as possible, at as early an age as possible.

4 ~ Avoid using food as a reward or comfort food, especially unhealthy foods.

5 – Be an example by *Eating for Health* regularly yourself and ask them to help keep you on track—fair is fair!

6 ~ Don't keep tempting junk food in the house. Do keep plenty of healthy foods and snacks on hand.

7 ~ Make a fun game out of exploring new healthy alternatives to unhealthy habits by taste testing new foods and finding ones that they like.

8 ~ Encourage other parents, teachers and family members to make healthy foods available at school and social functions.

9 ~ Have them take the *Symptoms Questionnaire* to help make the association between what they eat and how they feel. Or have them record how they feel before and after eating a generous amount of sugar or fast-food, for example.

10 ~ Pack a bag with nutritious foods when going out, and avoid having to resort to poor quality food choices for the sake of convenience and availability.

11 ~ Have a heart-to-heart talk with children and let them participate in decision making before you begin. Make incremental changes and establish them as lifestyle habits.

12 ~ Read *Try It, You'll Like It!* in this section and implement the "5 bites, 5 times" method of developing tastes for healthier foods.

book recommendations

- *Eat Healthy, Feel Great!*, Dr. William Sears

- *The Sneaky Chef: Simple Strategies for Hiding Healthy Foods in Kids Favorite Meals*, by Missy Chase Lapine

- *Little Sugar Addicts: End the Mood Swings, Meltdowns, Tantrums, and Low Self-Esteem in Your Child Today*, by Kathleen Desmaisons

- *Healthy Child, Healthy World*, by Robyn O'Brien (March, 2008) — Also visit her wesite: www.AllergyKids.com

section seven

Addendum
Assessments & Article Prescription Check List

Daily Food Diary Instructions & Form

List all food, drink, supplements (herbs, vitamins, etc.), prescription and over-the-counter drugs you ingest for 3-5 days. Include all snacks and condiments (i.e. mayonnaise, ketchup, salad dressing, etc.) indicating the brand names when applicable. Include at least one weekend day if you eat differently on the weekend. Eat what you normally eat and be honest.

The food you eat has a powerful impact on you as a whole. View the food diary as an opportunity to be an objective observer and increase awareness of your body, mind and spirit. While keeping the food diary, in addition to physical symptoms, pay attention to all aspects of your life, i.e. sleeping patterns, moods, interactions and relationships with others, self-talk, outlook on life, reactions to situations, etc. You may like to keep a separate journal for this.

While this is not required, great insight may be gained by doing so, especially when you take the next step and start to make changes in your diet. You can then get a much clearer idea of what foods are nourishing and supportive to your body at this time in your life and which foods are not.

Make blank copies of the food diary form on the next page. Make one copy for each of the days you intend to record what you eat. Please list all supplements and medications you're taking in the designated area below.

supplements or herbal formulas:

_____   _____
_____   _____
_____   _____

prescription medications:

_____   _____
_____   _____
_____   _____

over-the-counter medications:

_____   _____
_____   _____
_____   _____

No-Nonsense Nutrition

Article Series ~ By Kelly Hayford, CNC, Author *If It's Not Food, Don't Eat It!*

There isn't any condition in the body that can't be improved by improving your diet!

Day __	Time:	Daily Food Diary for: _____
morning	___ ___ ___ ___ ___	_____ _____ _____ _____ _____ _____ _____ _____
afternoon	___ ___ ___ ___	_____ _____ _____ _____ _____ _____ _____ _____
evening	___ ___ ___ ___	_____ _____ _____ _____ _____ _____ _____ _____
Day __	Time:	Symptoms Notes
	___ ___ ___	_____ _____ _____ _____ _____ _____

Note: *Make blank copies of this page for each of the 3-5 days you intend to keep a food diary.*

No-Nonsense Nutrition

Article Series ~ By Kelly Hayford, CNC, Author *If It's Not Food, Don't Eat It!*

Symptoms Questionnaire
Assessing the State of Your Health

name _____ date _____

☐ Initial Test: *the past 30 days*

☐ Retest: *the past 48 hours*   ☐ Other: *please specify* _____

Answering the *Symptoms Questionnaire* is a great way to quantitatively assess what's going on in your system at any given time. It's also a great tool to use when making changes to your diet to get a clear indication of the results you're getting.

For example, take the initial test 48 hours *before* you go off extreme, stimulants such as coffee or sugar. Then test 48 hours *after* you've been off these health-robbing substances and see the difference. Or, take the initial test right before you begin a 21-day *Basic Elimination Diet* or other cleansing program. Then take the test again after the first five days, then every week to monitor your progress.

point scale

0 = *Rarely* or *never* have the symptom
1 = Have it *occasionally*, but *not severe*
2 = Have it *occasionally* and is *severe*
3 = Have it *frequently*, but *not severe*

---

head
___ headaches
___ faintness
___ dizziness
___ insomnia
                              total ___

ears
___ itchy ears
___ earaches or ear infections
___ drainage from ear
___ ringing in ears or hearing loss
                              total ___

skin
___ acne, psoriasis, eczema, rosacea
___ hives, rashes, dry skin
___ hair loss
___ flushing or hot flashes
___ excessive sweating, not sweating
                              total ___

eyes
___ watery or itchy
___ swollen, reddened
___ sticky eyelids
___ bags or dark circles
___ blurred or tunnel vision
    (doesn't include near- or far-sightedness)
                              total ___

nose
___ stuffy nose, congestion
___ sinus problems
___ hay fever
___ sneezing attacks
___ excess mucous, sinus drainage
                              total ___

total this page _____

Continue on next page...

mouth/throat

___ chronic cough
___ frequent need to clear throat
___ sore throat, hoarseness, voice loss
___ swollen or discolored tongue, gums, lips
___ swollen tonsils
___ canker sores

total ____

muscles & joints

___ joint aches, pains
___ arthritis, fibromyalgia
___ stiffness or limited movement
___ muscular aches, pains
___ muscle weakness or fatigue

total ____

weight

___ binge eating or drinking
___ cravings for certain foods
___ excess weight
___ underweight
___ water retention

total ____

energy

___ fatigue, sluggishness
___ lethargy, apathy
___ hyperactive
___ restlessness
___ frequent colds & flu, illness

total ____

heart

___ irregular or skipped heart beat
___ rapid or pounding heart
___ high blood pressure
___ chest pain

total ____

lungs

___ chest congestion
___ asthma, bronchitis
___ shortness of breath
___ difficulty breathing

total ____

digestion & elimination

___ nausea, vomiting
___ diarrhea
___ constipation, straining
___ bloated belly
___ burping, passing gas
___ heartburn, acid reflux
___ stomach or intestinal pain
___ itchy anus, genital itch or discharge
___ frequent or urgent urination

total ____

emotions

___ mood swings
___ anxiety, fear, nervousness
___ anger, irritability, aggressiveness
___ depression

total ____

mind

___ difficulty making decisions
___ poor concentration, foggy brain
___ poor memory
___ confusion, poor comprehension
___ poor physical coordination
___ learning disabilities, autism
___ slurred speech
___ stuttering

total ____

_____

Total this page   _____
Total other side   _____

grand total   _____

evaluating your score

0-50 points.......Significant only if 10 or more points in any one system/organ category
51-75 points......Early indication of need for cleansing/dietary & lifestyle changes
76-100 points....Chronic toxicity, indicates a clear need for cleansing/dietary & lifestyle changes
101 & above......Chronic toxicity with acute conditions, indicates need for deep cleansing/
detoxification and immediate dietary & lifestyle changes.

No-Nonsense Nutrition

Article Series ~ By Kelly Hayford, CNC, Author *If It's Not Food, Don't Eat It!*

Section 7, No. 3

Copyright 2008
Kelly Hayford

Wellness Inventory

The *Wellness Inventory* consists of 100 items concerning your overall state of well-being. It is formulated to indicate where you currently are and to be done again at certain intervals to track your progress over time. You'll see a direct correlation between your inventory score and your level of wellness. As your inventory score increases, so too, will your overall health and well-being.

Each statement describes what many believe to be a wellness attribute. Because much wellness information is subjective and not able to be proven by current scientific methods, you and other healthcare providers may not agree on the specifics. In which case, you're invited to consider other possibilities to your currently held beliefs and to keep an open mind until you have had a chance to investigate further. Then you can make up your own mind from an informed perspective.

instructions

step 1 ~ make copies
Before you begin, be sure to make copies of each of the pages from these originals so you always have a clean copy for future use.

step 2 ~ answer each question
If true, check the box marked *True*. Be honest and challenge yourself. If the statement is usually or sometimes true, do not check the *True* box until the statement is virtually always true for you. Don't give yourself credit until it is really true. If the statement does not apply to you, check the *True* box.

step 3 ~ total each question
Add up the number of *True* boxes checked for each of the four sections and write the total at the bottom in the space provided. Then add together all four sections and write your current total in the box next to the *Progress Chart*.

step 4 ~ color in the progress chart
If you have 12 *True's* for the *Body* section, color in the bottom 12 boxes, and so on for each section. Always start from the bottom up. The goal is to eventually have as much of the chart filled in as possible. In the mean time, you'll have an idea of how you're doing in each of the four areas. Use a different color each time you take the inventory.

step 5 ~ repeat inventory regularly until all boxes are filled
You can do it! It may take 30 days or 365, but you can achieve a 80-100% score on your *Wellness Inventory*. It's a good idea to redo the *Wellness Inventory* at regular intervals—once a month, once every 3 months, etc. You decide what works best for you and work at your own pace. Keep in mind, that small gradual, integrated changes over time are longer lasting and easier to accomplish than quick, drastic changes, which can be overwhelming and lead to discouragement or abandonment of the program altogether. Also, know that you will vacillate from time to time. The goal isn't to be perfect 100% of the time, but to do *your best* as much of the time as possible.

There isn't any condition in the body that can't be improved by improving your diet!

Date _____

Total Score _____

Color _____

notes:

_____

_____

_____

_____

_____

_____

_____

_____

_____

_____

_____

_____

_____

_____

_____

_____

_____

_____

_____

_____

_____

_____

_____

true's	body	mind	spirit	enviro.
25				
24				
23				
22				
21				
20				
19				
18				
17				
16				
15				
14				
13				
12				
11				
10				
9				
8				
7				
6				
5				
4				
3				
2				
1				

body

- ❑ My weight is within average range.
- ❑ I walk or exercise 3-5 times a week.
- ❑ I have no need for medications or drugs (including prescription drugs).
- ❑ I drink plenty of *purified* water daily.
- ❑ I do conscious diaphragmatic breathing daily.
- ❑ I do not smoke or chew tobacco.
- ❑ I do not use illegal drugs or misuse prescription drugs.
- ❑ I rarely if ever experience gas, bloating, belching or other discomfort after I eat.
- ❑ I have healthy sleeping patterns and awaken refreshed and energetic.
- ❑ My hair and nails are healthy and look good.
- ❑ I rarely consume caffeine (coffee, chocolate, colas, tea). 0-4 times per month.
- ❑ I rarely consume alcohol, 0-3 times per month.
- ❑ I rarely consume foods made with concentrated sweetener, 0-2 times per week.
- ❑ I rarely consume refined white sugar, 0-2 times per month.
- ❑ I rarely consume white refined flour, 0-2 times per week.
- ❑ I am aware of any food sensitivities I have and I rarely eat those foods.
- ❑ I do not eat processed foods containing artificial preservatives, color, flavor or MSG.
- ❑ I use unrefined salt, i.e. sea salt, pink salt, etc.
- ❑ I eat a wide range of fresh fruits, vegetables, and whole grains daily.
- ❑ When making food choices, nourishing my body is my priority, not satisfying my taste-buds.
- ❑ I have a healthy (bulky and floats) bowel movement at least 1-3 times a day.
- ❑ I regularly flush my lymphatic system (i.e. by dry skin brushing, trampoline, massage, etc.).
- ❑ I have healthy teeth and gums.
- ❑ I am usually energetic and able to go throughout the day without fatigue.
- ❑ My skin and eyes are clear and vibrant.

_____ **number of true** *(25 possible)*

mind

- ❑ I take time to myself.
- ❑ I am creating the life I want instead of going with whatever comes along.
- ❑ I am open to many possibilities, rather than adhering to one perception or system.
- ❑ I believe that how I think and act contributes to my health and well-being.
- ❑ I read educational and inspirational materials regularly.
- ❑ I am in charge of my thoughts.
- ❑ It is easy for me to concentrate.
- ❑ I am aware that my perceptions of the world are affected by my thoughts at the time.
- ❑ I am aware that feelings provide me with information about myself and use them accordingly.
- ❑ I like myself/look forward to the rest of my life.
- ❑ I can ask for help when needed.
- ❑ I use healthcare practitioners as consultants, rather than following their instructions without question.
- ❑ I influence the rate of recovery from an illness.
- ❑ I am aware of internal contradictions among my thoughts and beliefs.
- ❑ I do not gossip or talk about others.
- ❑ I do not judge or criticize others.
- ❑ I make requests rather than complain to others.
- ❑ I am in tune with my wants and needs and get them taken care of.
- ❑ I do not criticize or put myself down outwardly or inwardly.
- ❑ Even when faced with serious challenges, I have the belief that it will all work out.
- ❑ I take responsibility for my actions and make amends when appropriate.
- ❑ I graciously receive compliments from others.
- ❑ I am aware of my own processes and patterns, and I am able to view myself objectively.
- ❑ I am aware of the power of my thoughts and words and choose both according to my desired outcome.
- ❑ I am aware that the sum total of each choice I make determines the overall course of my life.

_____ **number of true** *(25 possible)*

164

spirit

- ❑ I am curious about the nature of reality.
- ❑ I consider myself to be an integral part of a greater whole.
- ❑ I see myself reflected in others.
- ❑ I am aware that there is an order or balance to the universe.
- ❑ I take time daily to connect with my inner self.
- ❑ I am aware of my intuition and listen to its messages.
- ❑ I use prayer or meditation to reconnect with my inner self when things are out of balance.
- ❑ I view problems as opportunities to learn.
- ❑ When ill, I am able to consciously activate and speed up my healing processes.
- ❑ I can consciously alter my physiologic processes (muscle tension, circulation to part of body, etc.)
- ❑ The concept of God (may substitute word of choice) has personal meaning to me.
- ❑ I am aware of a part of me that is greater than my mind, body and emotions.
- ❑ I allow others to believe what they want and do not judge them for their beliefs.
- ❑ I am aware that my life has a greater purpose.
- ❑ I am fulfilling that greater purpose.
- ❑ My life has meaning and direction (although I may not always be able to see either).
- ❑ I have goals in my life.
- ❑ I am achieving those goals.
- ❑ My thoughts are primarily in the here and now rather than in the past or future.
- ❑ It is O.K. with me if certain things are unknowable to the mind.
- ❑ I experience a sense of wonder and awe when I contemplate the universe.
- ❑ Although I may not like it, I am aware that confusion and paradox are necessary for my growth.
- ❑ I do things that I love to do daily.
- ❑ I experience synchronistic events in my life.
- ❑ I believe that how I think and act contributes to the well-being of myself, others and the planet.

_____ **number of true** *(25 possible)*

environment

- ❑ I use household cleaners that do not contain harmful chemicals.
- ❑ I use personal care products free of harmful chemicals, and artificial colors/fragrances.
- ❑ I am surrounded by colors that I love.
- ❑ I am surrounded by beautiful things I love.
- ❑ I have healthy pets and plants.
- ❑ I wear clothes that I love and are neat, clean and make me look my best.
- ❑ My home is neat and clean (vacuumed, dusted, desks and tables are clear, etc.)
- ❑ My personal files, papers and receipts are regularly filed away.
- ❑ I live in the geographic area of my choice.
- ❑ My work environment is productive and inspirational (i.e. ample tools/resources, no undue pressure, etc.)
- ❑ My home and work space are free of clutter (including closets, under beds, cabinets, storage spaces, etc.)
- ❑ I regularly purge my environment of things I no longer need or use.
- ❑ I feel safe and comfortable in my environment.
- ❑ My bedroom is conducive to the best sleep possible.
- ❑ My car is in good running condition, neat and clean.
- ❑ I have nothing that is broken or in need of repair in my environment.
- ❑ My environment is free of major power lines.
- ❑ My pets are safe/comfortable in their home.
- ❑ I make my bed daily.
- ❑ Other people feel comfortable in my home.
- ❑ I am usually early or on time.
- ❑ I do not rush or use adrenaline to get things done.
- ❑ I love the people and pets that live with me.
- ❑ I am not stressed or damaged by my environment.
- ❑ I have regular quiet time in my space.

_____ **number of true** *(25 possible)*

ARTICLE PRESCRIPTION CHECKLIST

Name: _____

section 1 ~ Eating-for-Health Guideline #1:
If It's Not Food, Don't Eat It!

- ❏ No. 1 ~ If It's Not Food, Don't Eat It! - *No-Nonsense Guidelines to an EFH Lifestyle*
- ❏ No. 2 ~ Eating-for-Health Guideline #1: *If It's Not Food, Don't Eat It!*
- ❏ No. 3 ~ Health-Robbing Things to Avoid
- ❏ No. 4 ~ Harmful Food Additives to Avoid
- ❏ No. 5 ~ MSG: *The Hidden Health Robber*
- ❏ No. 6 ~ MSG: *Remedies & Resources*
- ❏ No. 7 ~ Hormones, Pesticides & GMO's
- ❏ No. 8 ~ Making the Transition to Natural Brand Foods
- ❏ No. 9 ~ Dietary Basics
- ❏ No. 10 ~ Healthy Habits
- ❏ No. 11 ~ Bottled Water: *Full of Health or Hype?*

section 2 ~ Eating-for-Health Guideline #1:
Eliminate or Relegate Stimulants to Rare Occasions

- ❏ No. 1 ~ Guideline #2: *Eliminate or Relegate Stimulants to Rare Occasions*
- ❏ No. 2 ~ Breaking Free of Stimulants:
- ❏ No. 3 ~ The Sugar Beast
- ❏ No. 4 ~ Alternatives to Coffee
- ❏ No. 5 ~ Curb & Conquer Food Cravings

section 3 ~ Guideline #3:
Eat an Abundance of Whole, Fresh, Natural Foods

- ❏ No. 1 ~ Eating-for-Health Guideline #3: *Eat an Abundance of Whole, Fresh, Natural Foods*
- ❏ No. 2 ~ Suggested Fruits & Vegetables
- ❏ No. 3 ~ Suggested Whole Grains
- ❏ No. 4 ~ Suggested Fats, Oils, Nuts & Seeds
- ❏ No. 5 ~ Suggested Meats, Fish, Poultry, Beans
- ❏ No. 6 ~ Natural Sweeteners
- ❏ No. 7 ~ Suggested Herbs, Spices & Dressings
- ❏ No. 8 ~ Whole Food Supplements: *An Essential Part of Today's Healthy Diet*
- ❏ No. 9 ~ How to Choose Whole-Food Supplement
- ❏ No. 10 ~ The Power of Fruits & Vegetables
- ❏ No. 11 ~ What About Organic?

section 4 ~ Guideline #4:
Account for Food Allergies & Sensitivities

- ❏ No. 1 ~ Eating-for-Health Guideline #4: *Account for Food Allergies & Sensitivities*
- ❏ No. 2 ~ Wheat: *A Problem Food for EveryBody*
- ❏ No. 3 ~ Got Milk or Dairy Products? - *Why You May Want to Eliminate or Limit Them*
- ❏ No. 4 ~ Soy — Oh, Boy! - *Things to Consider About This Not-Always-Healthy Health Food*
- ❏ No. 5 ~ Basic Elimination Diet Part 1: *Clear Cravings & Identify Food Sensitivities*
- ❏ No. 6 ~ Basic Elimination Diet Part 2: *What to Eat?*
- ❏ No. 7 ~ Food Allergy Testing Instructions

section 5 ~ Guideline #5:
Account for Ailments When Making Food Choices

- ❏ No. 1 ~ Eating-for-Health Guideline #5: *Account for Ailments When Making Choices*
- ❏ No. 2 ~ Finding Your Natural Weight
- ❏ No. 3 ~ Improving Digestion & Elimination
- ❏ No. 4 ~ Cleanse & Clear Your System
- ❏ No. 5 ~ Enema Instructions
- ❏ No. 6 ~ Cold & Flu Busters
- ❏ No. 7 ~ Emotional Eating

section 6 ~ Make It So!
Tips for Making Eating for Health a Reality

- ❏ No. 1 ~ Kitchen Set Up/ Food Shopping Tips
- ❏ No. 2 ~ Menu Planning & Making Healthy Foods Available
- ❏ No. 3 ~ Getting More Vegetables in Your Diet
- ❏ No. 4 ~ Eating Healthy When Eating Out
- ❏ No. 5 ~ Overcoming Obstacles Part 1 – *Intro / It Takes Too Much Time!*
- ❏ No. 6 ~ Overcoming Obstacles Part 2: *It's Too Expensive!*
- ❏ No. 7 ~ Overcoming Obstacles Part 3: *It's NO Fun!*
- ❏ No. 8 ~ Overcoming Part 4: *It's Too Hard!*
- ❏ No. 9 ~ "The Talk" for Gaining Support: *Tips for a Heart-to-Heart with Loved Ones*
- ❏ No. 10 ~ Try It, You'll Like It! - *Training Your Taste Buds to Enjoy Real Food*
- ❏ No. 11 ~ Helping Children Eat Healthier

section 7 ~ Addendum
Tips for Making Eating for Health a Reality

- ❏ No. 1 ~ Food Diary Instructions & Form
- ❏ No. 2 ~ Symptoms Questionnaire: *Assessing the State of Your Health*
- ❏ No. 3 ~ Wellness Inventory
- ❏ *Article Prescription Check List*